Trainer's Guide

caring for
infants &
toddlers second edition

Diane Trister Dodge

Sherrie Rudick

Derry G. Koralek

Teaching Strategies Inc.
Washington, DC

Editor: Laurie Taub
Cover, book design, and computer illustrations: Carla Uriona
Production: Jennifer Love King

Teaching Strategies, Inc.
P.O. Box 42243
Washington, DC 20015
www.TeachingStrategies.com
ISBN 13: 978-1-879537-51-4
ISBN 10: 1-879537-51-6

Library of Congress Control Number: 2005924655

Printed and bound in the United States of America
2010   2009   2008   2007   2006
10 9 8 7 6 5 4 3 2

Table of Contents

Introduction

Caring for Infants & Toddlers is one in a series of competency-based training programs for child development center staffs and family child care providers who work with children from infancy through school age. It includes two resources for teachers: *Caring for Infants & Toddlers*, the book that contains all the readings for the 13 modules in the training program, and a *Skill-Building Journal* that guides teachers in applying what they learned from the reading. Each of the modules addresses the knowledge and skills related to one of the functional areas of the Child Development Associate (CDA) Competency Standards: Safe, Healthy, Learning Environment, Physical, Cognitive, Communication, Creative, Self, Social, Guidance, Families, Program Management, and Professionalism. The training program also includes this *Trainer's Guide*, which is designed for those who oversee and provide feedback to teachers as they complete the modules.

Caring for Infants & Toddlers introduces the core knowledge and skills that teachers need in order to provide high-quality programs for infants and toddlers. We use the term *teacher* to mean any adult who works with young children in a classroom setting, including mentor teachers, lead teachers, teacher aides, teacher assistants, caregivers, care providers, and volunteers.

Although there is a direct link between the training program and a developmentally appropriate curriculum, *Caring for Infants & Toddlers* does not take the place of a curriculum. Early childhood programs should have a written curriculum that defines the program's philosophy, is based on research and theory, outlines goals for children's development and learning, and explains what children will learn (the content). The curriculum should also explain how teachers create a learning environment, guide children's learning, assess learning and development, and promote the meaningful involvement of families as partners in children's learning. All the modules in *Caring for Infants & Toddlers* help teachers develop the skills and knowledge to effectively implement their program's curriculum.

Caring for Infants & Toddlers is designed as a supervised, self-instructional training program. Teachers may work on the 13 modules in any order, at their own paces, and at times that are convenient for them. Trainers play a central role in overseeing the training, tracking teachers' progress, and assessing teachers' competence. Trainers observe teachers working with children, model appropriate practices, and provide feedback and support. They review and make judgments about teachers' responses in the learning activities. When a teacher has successfully completed all of the sections of a module, the trainer gives the knowledge assessments and observes the teacher to assess his or her competence in working with children, families, and colleagues.

While the training program is designed to be individualized and self-instructional, the materials are flexible enough to be used in a variety of other ways. For example, the modules can be the focus of a series of workshops offered by a training organization such as a resource and referral agency. Child development programs can use the modules as their in-house training program and discuss learning activities at staff meetings or at scheduled professional development sessions. Colleges can use selected modules in *Caring for Infants & Toddlers* as a textbook for a range of early childhood courses.

Key Features of the Training Program

Caring for Infants & Toddlers is a unique training program. The approach incorporates several key features that are critical to its success.

Training is individualized. *Caring for Infants & Toddlers* can be used by new or experienced teachers to increase their knowledge and understanding of infants and toddlers and developmentally appropriate practice. The *Self-Assessment* and the *Pre-Training Assessments* are designed to acknowledge and build on each teacher's existing skills and knowledge. The module-completion plan (for which a form is included in the Appendix) allows teachers and trainers to set individual schedules for completing the modules. The learning activities invite teachers to make choices, e.g., which child to observe, what activity to plan and implement, when to use a checklist, what part of the environment to assess and improve. Teachers are encouraged to think critically and reflect on their own performance. They also help determine when they are ready to be assessed.

Teachers receive ongoing feedback on the basis of regular, systematic observations. While much of the training is self-directed, the role of the trainer is critical to teachers' skill development and the application of knowledge. Trainers observe teachers working with children, give feedback based on those observations, model appropriate practices, and discuss completed learning activities.

The training involves hands-on learning. Most of the learning activities enable teachers to develop skills while applying knowledge on the job. Teachers develop, implement, and evaluate plans with colleagues. They build partnerships with families, use observation notes to individualize their programs, and complete checklists to identify and address problems.

The training is competency-based. Knowledge and competency assessments are built into the training process. The assessments provide concrete validation of each teacher's growth and learning of core competencies.

How to Use the Trainer's Guide

The *Trainer's Guide to Caring for Infants & Toddlers* provides guidance on using the modules for individualized training and in workshops and courses. The chapters lead trainers through the process of planning and overseeing the training program.

Chapter 1, *Planning Staff Development*, describes adult learners and the importance of counting all training toward professional development. It identifies the components of a career development system and shows how this training program leads to professional development and program improvement.

Chapter 2, *Supporting the Self-Instructional Training Process*, provides an overview of the trainer's role in introducing the training program and providing feedback to teachers as they complete each section of the modules. It describes exactly what teachers and trainers do to complete each module and suggests strategies to extend learning.

Chapter 3, *Using the Modules in Courses and Workshops*, is for trainers who will implement *Caring for Infants & Toddlers* in group settings such as workshops, seminars, or college courses. It offers suggestions about logistics, facilitating group training sessions, varying training approaches, and evaluating the effectiveness of training. A sample outline is provided for leading a series of group training sessions on module 6, *Communication*.

Chapter 4, *Assessing Each Teacher's Progress*, explains how to administer and score the knowledge and competency assessments and discuss the results. The *Knowledge Assessments*, *Answer Sheets*, and *Competency Assessments* are included at the end of this chapter.

The Appendix includes reproducible forms for planning the completion of modules, planning group sessions, tracking individual and group progress, documenting training, and evaluating training. There is also a certificate of completion to award to teachers when they finish all of the modules in the training program.

Chapter 1

Planning Staff Development

Your decision to use *Caring for Infants & Toddlers* is a commitment to supporting the professional development of one or more classroom teachers who work with infants and toddlers. To accomplish this goal, you want the training you provide to result in increased competence and lead to career advancement for each teacher.

Effective training experiences exist within a context, not as isolated events. Just as a curriculum for young children is not simply a collection of activities, a series of workshops alone does not lead to professional growth and career advancement. The training you provide using *Caring for Infants & Toddlers* must address core competencies and fit an established system of career development that ensures that all training experiences are documented and lead to professional development. The training should also incorporate what is known about how adults learn best.

Considering How Adults Learn

The training design and approach for *Caring for Infants & Toddlers* are based on adult learning principles. Most adults are self-directed and want to be responsible for their own learning. How much they get out of training depends on how important the content is to them, how much effort they put into the learning process, and whether they integrate and use what they learn. Trainers need to consider adult motivation to learn and how feedback and other forms of support reflect principles of adult learning theory.

For most adults, motivation to learn is closely related to whether they can **immediately apply the knowledge and skills** being addressed. They want to know what they will be learning so they can determine whether it will be useful. This training program defines clear objectives in the *Self-Assessment* and *Pre-Training Assessments* and at the beginning of each learning activity. At each step, teachers can clearly see what they will be learning and how it relates to their work with children.

Adults view job-related learning as a means to an end, not an end in itself. They are motivated to participate in training that allows them to **develop or improve specific job-related skills**. *Caring for Infants & Toddlers* addresses this incentive because most of the learning activities are completed while working with children and families.

Time is a limited and valuable investment for working adults. They have more positive attitudes toward training when they believe the **time invested is well-spent**. The knowledge and skills gained through this training program will help teachers become more effective in their work with children. Trainers can reinforce this incentive by pointing out to teachers how their increased skills and knowledge are benefiting children.

A strong secondary factor related to an adult's motivation to learn is to **increase self-esteem and enjoyment of work**. This training program acknowledges and builds on what teachers already know. As they complete learning activities, modules, and the assessment process, teachers feel successful and competent. Teachers who know they are competent tend to enjoy their work and want to continue learning.

According to many studies, motivation increases with **recognition for achievements, respect for the individual as a person**, and **participation in planning and decision making**. The process for assessing teachers' knowledge and competency recognizes their accomplishments. The self-paced, individualized approach demonstrates respect for each person's unique training needs and strengths. There are many opportunities for teachers to plan and make decisions about their learning. The greatest incentive, however, is to tie training and demonstration of competence to salary increases.

Applying the Principles of Adult Learning Theory

Effective training experiences should be based on information about how adults learn best.

Adults bring a **wealth of previous experience** to training. They find training more meaningful when their life experience is recognized and when they can relate the content to their own lives. Each *Caring for Infants & Toddlers* module includes a section for teachers to relate the content to their own lives, and the *Pre-Training Assessments* allow them to rate their own use of strategies.

Adults need **opportunities to integrate new ideas with what they already know** so they can use the new information. Training should provide opportunities to make interpretations and draw conclusions. Many of the learning activities in this training program require teachers to answer questions about why they plan specific activities, how children react, what they might do differently in the future, and how they can build on what they learn.

Adults **acquire new concepts more slowly** than information that relates to something they already know. The self-paced nature of this training program allows enough time for teachers to learn and apply new concepts. In addition, because some learning activities build on previous ones, new concepts are repeated and reinforced.

Adults tend to **acquire information even more slowly when it conflicts with what they already know,** because it forces them to reevaluate their knowledge base. The trainer's feedback conferences with teachers are opportunities to discuss and evaluate new ideas.

Adults tend to **take errors personally,** and some find it **difficult to take risks.** This training program encourages reflection, critical thinking, and skill development rather than focusing on right or wrong answers. Teachers are encouraged to use the *Answer Sheets* as guides for learning, rather than view them as the only correct responses.

Adults **perceive their own experiences as unique and private.** They are not always comfortable or willing to share these experiences with others. Each teacher receives a copy of the *Skill-Building Journal,* which is a personal account of that individual's professional development. Trainers need to respect teachers' privacy while offering encouragement.

Adults learn best through a **hands-on approach** that involves them actively in the learning process. The learning activities in *Caring for Infants & Toddlers* are hands-on because they require teachers to use what they have read while caring for children and then to think and write about their experiences. Teachers' understanding is enhanced when trainers observe and provide feedback to teachers as they work with children and families.

Applying the Principles to Training

Principles of Adult Learning	What Trainers Can Do
Adults bring a wealth of experiences to training.	Use the *Self-Assessment* and *Pre-Training Assessments* to acknowledge what teachers already know and do.
Adults need time to integrate new information with what they already know.	Allow time for teachers to apply new ideas in their work and provide support and encouragement.
Adults need extra time to understand new information that doesn't relate to what they already know.	Respect the self-paced training approach so teachers have time to internalize new information.
Adults need even more time to integrate new information that conflicts with what they know.	Use feedback conferences to discuss and evaluate old and new knowledge.
Adults tend to take errors personally and some have difficulty taking risks.	Emphasize reflection and critical thinking rather than right or wrong answers.
Adults perceive their own experiences as unique and private.	Reassure teachers that the *Skill-Building Journal* is their personal record and sharing with others is their choice.
Adults learn best through a hands-on approach.	Observe teachers as they apply what they learn in their work with children and families. Provide support and resources for completing learning activities.

Making Training Count

The field of early childhood education is defined as "any part- or full-day group program in a center, school, or home that serves children from birth through age eight, including children with special developmental and learning needs."[1] It is a broad field that allows multiple entry points. Some teachers enter the profession from colleges and graduate schools with advanced degrees. Some begin preparing in high school vocational programs. Still others enter the field with no professional preparation, credential, or degree and gain professional knowledge and skills entirely on the job. Because the early childhood field includes diverse roles in a variety of settings, training experiences must accommodate many different levels of preparation, be cohesive, and lead to a credential or degree.

Today most states have established a comprehensive career development system for offering and tracking professional development experiences for early childhood educators. These organized systems ensure that all professional development experiences address the acquisition of specific skills and knowledge, lead to a certificate or credit toward a degree, and result in improved compensation and benefits. Several components of these systems are described in the chart on page 11.

A Core Body of Knowledge and Competencies

Every profession defines a specialized body of knowledge and competencies that all members of that profession are expected to have. Regardless of where they take place, training experiences for teachers of young children should address the core competencies defined by the early childhood profession.

In designing systems of professional development, most states have adopted or based their core competencies on the subject areas outlined by The Council for Professional Recognition.[2] This core body of knowledge and competencies recognizes that effective teachers of young children

- plan a safe, healthy learning environment

- advance children's physical and intellectual development

- support children's social and emotional development

- establish productive relationships with families

- manage and effective program operation

- maintain a commitment to professionalism

- observe and record children's behavior

- know and apply principles of child development and learning

These subject areas provide a blueprint for individual professional development and a way to assess progress. They are the basis for all training experiences. *Caring for Infants & Toddlers* addresses knowledge and competencies by organizing content around the 13 functional areas defined by The Council for Professional Recognition.

A Training Approval System

A second component of a comprehensive system of professional development is a training approval system to ensure that all training experiences meet quality standards and lead to professional development. A training approval system should include procedures for reviewing and validating workshops and conferences as eligible for continuing education units and college or graduate credit, categorizing college courses in terms of their relevance to licensing requirements and credentialing programs, and ensuring that training experiences meet requirements for specific training levels and topic areas.

In developing a training approval system, many states have followed a set of principles of effective professional development. As defined by NAEYC,[3] effective professional development experiences

- are part of an ongoing process allowing staff to continually incorporate and apply new knowledge and skills related to working with children and families

- are grounded in a sound theoretical and philosophical base and structured as a coherent and systematic program

- are responsive to an individual's background, experiences, and current role

- allow staff to see clear links between theory and practice

- use interactive, hands-on approaches that encourage staff to learn from one another

- contribute to positive self-esteem by acknowledging the skills and resources staff members bring to the training process

- provide opportunities for application and reflection and allow staff members to be observed and receive feedback about what they have learned

- encourage staff members to take responsibility for planning their own professional development program

The training approach used in *Caring for Infants & Toddlers* reflects and builds on these principles.

To ensure that training experiences meet these principles of effective professional development, many states now require individuals who offer training as part of the career development system to be certified. The criteria used to determine certification generally include

- knowledge, education, and experience in early childhood education and child development, including areas of specialization such as special needs, that qualify them to teach the content of the class

- knowledge of how adults learn, including demonstrated sensitivity to individual differences and learning styles

- sensitivity to cultural and linguistic diversity and to one's own cultural biases

- understanding of the early childhood profession and a commitment to professionalism

- knowledge of state and local regulations and requirements for programs and staff

Organizations that offer staff training—child care agencies, Head Start and Early Head Start programs, resource and referral agencies, Child and Adult Care Food Programs, Departments of Recreation, colleges, universities, schools—may also be required to meet criteria established by the state. Such criteria usually include ensuring that all their trainers meet established qualifications; that training meets the requirements for licensing, certification, credentialing, or a degree in early childhood education; and that the content of training is based on accepted theories and practices in early childhood education and addresses the core competencies identified by the early childhood profession. Additionally, organizations must set up a system for documenting the training provided (e.g., transcripts, certificates of attendance) and maintain a permanent record of attendance at the training sessions.

A Personnel Registry

A third essential component of a professional development system is a centralized tracking system to document all training completed by individuals in the profession. Documentation of training can include official transcripts from a college or university, a certificate of participation from an organization providing training that is signed by the trainer or a representative from the sponsoring group, or an official form provided at a conference or training session, with appropriate safeguards to ensure validation of each person's participation. Documentation forms, such as the Training Record included in the Appendix of this *Trainer's Guide*, become part of a teacher's permanent record. Documentation must include

- the participant's name

- the title of the workshop, course, or seminar, and the competency area addressed

- training date(s)

- total number of hours of training completed, including designation of clock hours or credit hours (and the number of clock hours which constitute one credit hour)

- signature or stamp of the instructor or program administrator

A permanent registry for training records is essential to professional development for several reasons. Many states have staff training requirements built into licensing standards. Centers must keep these records, but they should also be maintained in a centralized and permanent location. Increasingly, colleges and universities give college credit for documented training experiences by certified trainers that address the profession's standards but are not part of the regular college program. Thus training experiences can lead to an AA degree, which is necessary for career development.

Caring for Infants & Toddlers can be an effective tool for promoting professional growth. The 13 modules in the training program can be applied to obtaining a Child Development Associate (CDA) Credential or program accreditation.

A CDA Credential: The First Step in Professional Development

The Child Development Associate National Credentialing Program is a major effort to provide early childhood educators with a credential based on demonstrated competency. The program began in 1971 with the goal of enhancing the quality of early childhood education by improving, evaluating, and recognizing the competence of individuals who work with children from birth to age five in center-based and family child care settings.

The Council for Professional Recognition establishes the policies and sets the standards for the credentialing program and awards the CDA Credential. The Council awards a CDA Credential to adults who demonstrate competence in caring for young children. To date, nearly 85,000 early care and education workers have received a CDA Credential.

There are two routes to obtaining a CDA Credential: Direct Assessment and the Professional Preparation Program. To apply through Direct Assessment, a candidate must document completion of 120 clock hours of training with no less than ten hours in each of the eight subject areas defined by the profession. Formal training may be provided by training specialists, Head Start or child care agencies, colleges, vocational or technical schools, or resource and referral agencies, and it must cover the specific subject areas outlined by the Council. Completion of the 13 modules in *Caring for Infants & Toddlers* enables teachers to meet or exceed the Council's training requirements. (A sample form for documenting contact hours can be found in the Appendix.)

Teachers applying for a Credential are responsible for developing a Professional Resource File, which is a collection of documents to use in working with children and families. The learning activities in *Caring for Infants & Toddlers* include many opportunities for teachers to document work and collect materials for their Professional Resource File.

Direct Assessment also requires teachers to complete a written and oral assessment and to be observed working directly with children. The knowledge and competency assessments that complete each module will help teachers prepare for the CDA assessments.

In the second route to obtaining a CDA Credential, the Council arranges for teachers to enter a college-level Professional Preparation Program, which offers training and assessment using the Council's curriculum, *Essentials*. There are three phases in the CDA Professional Preparation Program: field work, instructional course work, and evaluation.

To keep up-to-date on the process for obtaining a CDA Credential, contact The Council for Professional Recognition at (800) 424-4310 or log on to their Web site (www.cdacouncil.org).

Using the Modules for Program Improvement

An increasing body of research identifies a link between training, program quality, and positive outcomes for children. The National Child Care Staffing Study suggests that accredited centers provide higher-than-average-quality services. "The accredited centers had better-compensated teachers with more formal education and specialized early childhood training, provided better benefits and working conditions, and maintained lower rates of turnover."[4]

Unfortunately, most state regulations fall far short of ensuring that programs meet standards of quality that all children need to thrive. Welfare reform poses new challenges to the profession as some states consider lowering standards for programs and staff qualifications in order to expand child care services.

One of the benefits of using a comprehensive training program for all staff is that the quality of the program is enhanced as teachers gain new skills and knowledge that they apply to their work. Program accreditation is a voluntary approach for recognizing and promoting high-quality programs serving young children. The accreditation process can be a powerful motivator for everyone working at a site to come together and work toward program improvement.

Accreditation begins with an extensive self-study process focusing on established criteria. All program staff members and parents complete forms to evaluate the program and identify areas where improvement is needed. Many of the trainers and directors who use *Caring for Infants & Toddlers* review the results of this self-assessment process when selecting which modules to introduce to teachers first. For example, if a program does not meet the standards for promoting children's health, all teachers can begin with Module 2, *Healthy*, and discuss each section as a group.

When program staff members think they have met all the criteria, they submit their paperwork to the accrediting organization. This organization arranges a site visit by a validator who verifies the accuracy of the program's self-assessment. The validated self-assessment is reviewed by a commission, or board, that has the power to grant accreditation for a specified period of years, or to defer accreditation and make recommendations on areas that must be improved first. Two main organizations provide accreditation for center-based programs.[5]

The National Academy of Early Childhood Programs, a division of NAEYC, administers a national, voluntary, professionally sponsored accreditation system for programs serving children from birth through kindergarten. Since establishing the system in 1985, NAEYC has accredited more than 8100 programs serving approximately three-quarters of a million young children and their families.

NAEYC National Academy of Early Childhood Programs
1509 16th Street, N.W.
Washington, DC 20036
(800) 424-2460 or (202) 232-8777
www.naeyc.org

The National Early Childhood Program Accreditation (NECPA) is an independent voluntary accreditation program developed with the National Child Care Association, the largest organization of proprietary child care professionals. Since 1993, the NECPA has accredited 110 centers across the United States.

The National Early Childhood Program Accreditation Commission
126C Suber Road
Columbia, SC 29210
800-505-9878
www.necpa.net

The chart that follows shows how the modules in *Caring for Infants & Toddlers* might be grouped into a series of courses and how they address the CDA Subject Areas and NAEYC Early Childhood Program Standards. (Note: Beginning in late 2005, programs seeking NAEYC accreditation will have to demonstrate compliance with each of the program standards and criteria developed by the Commission on NAEYC Early Childhood Program Standards and Accreditation Criteria.)

---

[1] National Association for the Education of Young Children. (1993). *A conceptual framework for early childhood professional development.* Washington, DC: Author.

[2] The Council for Professional Recognition. (1996). *The child development associate assessment system and competency standards: Preschool caregivers in center-based programs.* Washington, DC: Author.

[3] Op cit.

[4] Whitebrook, M. (1996). NAEYC accreditation as an indicator of program quality: What research tells us. In S. Bredekamp & B. Willer (Eds.), *NAEYC accreditation: A decade of learning and the years ahead* (p. 35). Washington, DC: National Association for the Education of Young Children.

[5] Stoney Associates. (1996). Accreditation as a quality improvement strategy. In *Building and maintaining an effective child care/early education system in your state* (pp. 20-22). Albany, NY: Author.

Using *Caring for Infants & Toddlers* for
Professional Development and Program Improvement

Course Title	*Caring for Infants & Toddlers* Modules	Clock Hours	CDA Subject Areas Addressed	NAEYC Early Childhood Program Standards
Establishing the Environment	1-Safe	12	Planning a safe, healthy learning environment	Health, Physical Environment
	2-Healthy	12		
	3-Learning Environment	14		
Child Growth and Development: Cognitive and Physical	4-Physical	10	Steps to advance children's physical and intellectual development	Curriculum, Relationships, Teaching
	5-Cognitive	10		
	6-Communication	10	Principles of child growth and development	
	7-Creative	10		
Child Growth and Development: Social and Emotional	8-Self	11	Positive ways to support children's social and emotional development	Curriculum, Relationships, Teaching
	9-Social	11		
	10-Guidance	16	Principles of child growth and development	
Introduction to the Early Childhood Profession	11-Families	10	Strategies to establish productive relationships with families	Assessment, Teachers, Families, Communities, Leadership, and Management
	12-Program Management	20	Strategies to manage an effective program operation	
	13-Professionalism	10	Maintaining a commitment to professionalism	
			Observing and documenting children's behavior	
Applied Early Childhood Practices (lab or practicum)	This course would include observations of each student's application of material presented in class and provide individualized support and feedback.	16	Observations by an advisor are part of the CDA credentialing process	Site validator visit

Chapter 2

Supporting the Self-Instructional Training Process

The trainer is central to the success of this self-instructional training program. This chapter suggests ways to introduce the content and format of the training to teachers who will be using the modules. It explains your role in leading teachers through the *Orientation* and the steps of each module and offers suggestions about conducting feedback conferences so they are positive learning experiences.

At the end of this chapter you will find a chart describing what teachers do and what trainers do in each of the 13 modules. For each topic, we also suggest ways to extend learning.

Introducing the Training Program

In preparing to introduce the training program, make sure you have several copies of *Caring for Infants & Toddlers* that teachers may keep or share and a *Skill-Building Journal* for each teacher to keep. Plan to meet with teachers, individually or in small groups, so you can describe the training content and design and explain how you plan to support, assess, and document their progress.

You might begin by discussing what it means to be a competent teacher and explaining how the modules help teachers expand and build on their knowledge and skills in caring for infants and toddlers. Use the points that follow.

Competent teachers apply their knowledge of child development. They use what they know about infants and toddlers to plan for each child and for the group. The first learning activity in many of the modules summarizes the typical characteristics of infants and toddlers and describes how they are related to the topics addressed in the module. In addition, many learning activities include information about child development and opportunities to apply that knowledge while caring for young children.

Competent teachers establish strong partnerships with families. This training program recognizes parents as the prime educators of their children. In addition to completing module 11, *Families*, teachers involve families as they carry out and discuss learning activities in other modules. The modules emphasize the importance of offering a program that corresponds with the ethnicities, cultures, and languages of the children and their families.

Competent teachers document their systematic, objective observations. Observations allow teachers to learn about each child, measure children's progress, and evaluate program effectiveness. Information gathered through regular, systematic observations helps teachers learn about each child's needs, skills, interests, and individual characteristics. That information is shared with families and used to plan for the group and for individual children.

Competent teachers offer a program that meets individual needs. This topic is addressed in depth in module 12, *Program Management*. In addition, it is reinforced through many learning activities. Teachers observe and report what they learn about individual children. They use what they learn to make decisions about introducing new materials, rearranging the environment, tailoring their interactions, and sharing information with families.

Competent teachers take time to think about their practices. Reflection is an important part of most of the learning activities. Teachers plan, implement their ideas, and then report and evaluate what took place. They describe how they might change an activity if they offer it again, what materials they could provide to help a child gain specific skills, how to engage children through play, or ways to make the environment safer for children.

Discuss the Content and Approach

Describe how the modules address the 13 functional areas of the CDA Competencies and support the professional development of infant/toddler teachers. Refer teachers to the description of the 13 functional areas of the CDA Competencies that is provided in the *Orientation* and ask which topics and skills they would most like to learn about and in what order. Point out that *Caring for Infants & Toddlers* may be used flexibly; teachers may begin with whichever module is of most interest.

Invite teachers to think about how they learn best, what helps them gain knowledge and skills. Teachers may mention approaches such as classroom support and feedback by trainers, supervisors, or colleagues; viewing videotapes; reading books or articles; watching someone else perform a task; and discussing an idea or concept. Give specific examples that show how the *Caring for Infants & Toddlers* training approach incorporates these strategies.

Explain the Importance of Observing and Recording

Explain that teachers will conduct and document observations as they complete many of the learning activities in this training program. If possible, review and help teachers practice the skills used to conduct and record systematic, objective, accurate, and complete observations. As a resource, you can use *Learning Activity A, Getting to Know Each Child*, in module 12, *Program Management*.

Explain that you, too, will use observation as a tool. You will observe teachers throughout the training program to learn more about their skills and how you can help them continue to grow. Your observation notes will serve as the basis for providing objective feedback to teachers about their progress in applying knowledge and skills and for assessing their competence.

Describe Your Plan for Feedback Conferences

Describe how the training program is tailored to address individual needs and how it provides a close working relationship between trainer and teacher. Emphasize that, although teachers use the materials independently, they are not left alone to sink or swim. Regular feedback is an integral part of the training process. Describe the purpose and frequency of feedback conferences and the approach (one-on-one, teaching teams, or groups) you plan to use.

If you will be conducting group feedback meetings, explain that these are opportunities for teachers to discuss the learning activities and to support each other. Peer support encourages teachers as they work with children each day, and it contributes to their professional growth.

Distribute and review the "Individual Tracking Form" found in the Appendix. Encourage teachers to monitor their own progress. Note the space for the trainer to sign the form when each module is completed.

Acknowledge Teachers' Accomplishments

The competence teachers gain in their work with children and families as they complete the modules will be rewarding, itself. However, it makes a difference when the program they work for acknowledges their undertaking and completing the training program. If possible, let teachers know the program's plan for offering incentives.

Here are ways that some programs acknowledge and reward teachers' efforts.

- Award increases in salaries and benefits for successfully completing different levels of training.

- Offer a certificate for dinner for two donated by a local restaurant, a new material for the children, or a copy of a favorite resource when a teacher has successfully completed a certain number of modules.

- Show pictures to potential program applicants that highlight individual teachers interacting with children. Write brief summaries of teachers' special interests and accomplishments.

- Hold recognition dinners and award ceremonies for teachers who have completed the program. Invite spouses, parents, and other special guests.

- Offer child care so a teacher and guest can spend an evening out. Teachers might volunteer their child care services to acknowledge a colleague's success.

- Provide special pins, tote bags, or framed certificates that are concrete symbols of a teacher's completion of part or all of the training.

- Post on a bulletin board or include in the program newsletter photographs of teachers who have undertaken or completed the training.

Completing the *Orientation*

All teachers begin the training program by completing the *Orientation* that describes the value and special features of the training program, provides definitions of the 13 functional areas of the CDA Competencies, and explains the steps in the training process. The *Orientation* ends with a *Self-Assessment*, which lists three major areas of competence related to the topic of each module. Teachers should be encouraged to respond as objectively as possible so they can identify their strengths and interests, as well as areas that need strengthening.

Schedule a time to meet with each teacher to review the *Orientation* and the *Self-Assessment*. Allow enough time (15–30 minutes) to discuss the results and to develop a module-completion plan with the teacher. The plan lists the first three modules to work on, target completion dates, and a tentative schedule for completing the entire training program. Most teachers need about four weeks to complete the sections of a module. The entire training program generally takes 12–18 months to complete.

Try to give teachers substantial autonomy in developing the module-completion plan. Sometimes other factors influence which modules a teacher works on first. For example, the module-completion plan might consider program-wide improvement goals, such as reducing injuries or creating more effective learning environments. In such cases, all teachers would complete the same module so they can work together to achieve the program's goal.

Many trainers, especially those implementing the training program for the first time, find it helpful to have several teachers work on the same module at the same time. This way you can conduct group feedback sessions, and teachers can learn from and provide support to one another. Group sessions also make supervision less time-consuming, but keep in mind that one of the most valuable aspects of the training is the feedback you provide each teacher.

Completing a Module

Each of the 13 modules follows a consistent format using both *Caring for Infants & Toddlers* and the *Skill-Building Journal*. The chart that follows illustrates how the books are used.

Section	Caring for Infants & Toddlers	Skill-Building Journal
Overview	An introduction to the topic addressed in the module, identification of three major areas of competence, related strategies, and three brief examples of how teachers apply their knowledge and skills to support children's development and learning.	Questions about each of the examples and sample answers.
Your Own Experiences	A short discussion of how the topic applies to adults.	A series of questions about personal experiences related to the topic.
Pre-Training Assessment (presented only in the Skill-Building Journal)		A checklist of how often teachers use key strategies and a question about skills to improve or topics to learn more about.
Learning Activities (4–5 per module)	Objectives for each Learning Activity and several pages of information about the topic.	Instructions for applying the reading to classroom practices. This may involve answering questions; observing children and using the information to address individual needs and interests; completing a checklist; trying new teaching strategies; or planning, implementing, and evaluating a new activity. When appropriate, Answer Sheets are provided.
Reflecting on Your Learning (presented only in the Skill-Building Journal)		An opportunity to consider how the topic relates to curriculum implementation and building partnerships with families. Questions help teachers summarize what they learned.

Although the content and activities in the modules vary, teachers and trainers follow the same process for completing each one. The process for completing the sections of each module is described in the following paragraphs and illustrated in the diagram on page 21.

Overview

Teachers read about the topic addressed in the module. For each area of competence, they review strategies that teachers use and three examples of how teachers apply their knowledge and skills. Teachers answer questions about each example and compare their answers to those on the *Answer Sheets* in the *Skill-Building Journal* at the end of the module.

Your Own Experiences

Next, **teachers** answer questions about how the topic relates to their own experiences, both on and off the job. They examine how personal experiences affect their approaches to their work with children and families and their choice of teaching strategies.

Pre-Training Assessment

Teachers complete the *Pre-Training Assessment*—a list of the strategies that competent teachers use—by indicating whether they do these things regularly, sometimes, or not enough. They review their responses and identify 3–5 skills they want to improve or topics they want to learn more about. Teachers can refer to the *Glossary* at the end of *Caring for Infants & Toddlers* for definitions of the terms used.

The **trainer** schedules a time to meet with teachers to discuss the questions about the *Overview*, their own experiences, and the *Pre-Training Assessment*. You might point out what they will be learning and how their skills will be enhanced. **Teachers** then begin the learning activities for the module.

Learning Activities

Each module includes four or five learning activities. After reading several pages of information about the topic, **teachers** apply their knowledge while working with children and families. For example, they might answer questions related to the reading and their own teaching practices; complete a checklist; try suggestions from the reading and report the results; plan, implement, and evaluate an activity; or observe and record children's behavior and interactions and then use the observation notes to individualize the program. Examples of completed forms, summaries, and charts are provided, when needed, to explain the activity.

The **trainer,** when possible, offers support to teachers as they complete the learning activities. Support might include observing the teacher while he or she works with children, conducting a co-observation of a child, reviewing plans and assisting in collecting materials, or discussing and answering questions about the module content.

The **trainer** schedules a time to meet with teachers, individually or in a group, after they have completed the learning activities. Invite teachers to discuss the content and report what they did and learned. Provide additional feedback based on your observation notes and on the written portion of the learning activity: charts, checklists, plans, responses to questions, or observation summaries. For some activities, teachers meet with colleagues or a child's family, or review *Answer Sheets* at the end of the module.

Reflecting on Your Learning

After completing all of the learning activities, **teachers** summarize their progress. They review their responses to the *Pre-Training Assessment* and describe their increased knowledge and skills. For some modules, teachers also review and add examples to a chart created in one of the learning activities.

Teachers meet with their **trainer** to review their progress and to discuss whether they are ready for the knowledge and competency assessments. When teachers are ready, schedule times to administer the *Knowledge Assessment* and conduct the *Competency Assessment* observation. If a teacher needs to learn more about the knowledge and skills addressed in the module, suggest supplemental strategies.

For teachers who are having difficulty mastering the content, or for those who want to learn more about a specific topic, you can suggest other resources. Professional organizations and publishers offer numerous books, journals, videotapes, Web sites, and training manuals related to caring for infants and toddlers. *Caring for Infants & Toddlers* includes a bibliography of resources for early childhood professionals.

Assessing Knowledge and Competence

There is a *Knowledge Assessment* for each module and a *Competency Assessment* for modules 1–12. Chapter 4 of this *Trainer's Guide, Assessing Each Teacher's Progress*, describes the assessment process and offers guidance on administering, scoring, and discussing the results of the evaluations. It also includes the *Knowledge Assessments, Answer Sheets*, and the *Competency Assessment* observation forms.

Documenting Progress

As **teachers** successfully complete the learning activities and assessments, they can record their progress on the "Individual Tracking Form" (included in the Appendix) and ask for the trainer's signature. **Trainers** use the "Program Tracking Form" (in the Appendix) to document and monitor the progress of a group of teachers. Keeping this form up-to-date can help you schedule feedback sessions and assessments.

The Training Process

Complete the Orientation

Read about the training program
Complete the Self-Assessment
Develop a module-completion plan

Feedback
and
Discussion

Complete a Module

Overview

Read about the topic and three related areas of competence
Review examples of what teachers do
Answer questions

Your Own Experiences

Relate topic to own experiences
Answer questions

Pre-Training Assessment

Assess own use of strategies
List skills to improve or topics to learn about

Learning Activities

Read about topic
Apply knowledge
Answer questions

Reflecting on Your Learning

Review responses to Pre-Training Assessment
Summarize skills and knowledge gained
Discuss readiness for assessments

Feedback
and
Discussion

Not ready for assessment	**Ready for assessment**
Review or repeat activities	Schedule times

Assessments

Knowledge Assessment
Competency Assessment

Feedback
and
Discussion

Did not demonstrate competence	**Demonstrated competence**
Review or repeat activities	Document progress
	Begin next module

Providing Feedback

Whether provided one-on-one or during group sessions, your feedback to teachers is central to the success of the training program. Feedback conferences are particularly important because of the self-instructional nature of *Caring for Infants & Toddlers*. These conferences are opportunities for trainers to answer questions, offer support, make suggestions, listen to concerns, reinforce new skills, help teachers recognize how much they have learned, and encourage teachers to repeat activities they may have misunderstood the first time.

For each module, trainers provide feedback after teachers complete

- the *Overview*, *Your Own Experiences* (with the possible exception of module 3, *Healthy*, if teachers prefer to keep their responses private), and the *Pre-Training Assessment*

- each *Learning Activity*

- *Reflecting on Your Learning*

- the *Knowledge Assessment* and the *Competency Assessment*

Feedback conferences may be as short as 10 minutes or may last longer, depending on how much feedback and support teachers need. Try to schedule a feedback conference for each learning activity before the teacher begins the next one. It is always best to discuss responses while they are still fresh in the teacher's mind. A full understanding of each activity is particularly important when a learning activity builds on the knowledge and skills addressed in the previous one.

Encourage teachers to take the initiative in scheduling feedback conferences. You can post a schedule of times when you are available and encourage teachers to sign up when they are ready. When several teachers are working on the same module, a joint decision should be made about when to meet, because everyone will have to be on the same section of the module at the time of the feedback conference.

Here are some suggestions for conducting one-on-one or group feedback sessions. You may adapt them to reflect your own training style and what you know about each teacher.

Review the written responses to the section before the conference. This is especially important when preparing to give feedback on inappropriate responses. Consider how to offer constructive comments that encourage teachers to try an activity again.

Begin with an open-ended question. For example, you might ask, "What did you think about this activity?" or "What did you learn from this activity?" Take a few minutes to discuss each teacher's response to the question.

Use specific examples to acknowledge appropriate responses. For example, "The way you phrased that showed your respect for the child. You told him clearly what you expected, but you were careful to show him you understood his feelings."

Relate teachers' responses to information in the text. For example, "Your responses show that you understand how to use the suggested strategies for handling challenging behavior and why they are appropriate."

Ask questions about inappropriate responses. Instead of simply correcting them, help teachers think about why responses are inappropriate and how children might be affected. Open-ended questions, such as the following, are helpful:

- What are the reasons for the child's behavior?

- How could you involve the children in this routine?

- What message would this statement send to the child?

Help teachers arrive at appropriate responses. You might say, "Let's look at the text. Perhaps there's another way to phrase this so it offers guidance without making the child feel discouraged."

The underlying goal of providing feedback is to improve a teacher's skills and knowledge. If a teacher has not understood the information presented in a section, use the feedback conference to review and explain the information and promote understanding.

What Teachers and Trainers Do in Each Module

The following charts summarize what teachers and trainers do in each section of the 13 modules. Individual teachers and trainers have different learning and interaction styles. These charts therefore do not present hard-and-fast rules to be followed inflexibly. Rather, they summarize what teachers are asked to do and suggest constructive ways for trainers to provide support. Each chart is followed by suggested strategies for extending learning in individual or group sessions.

Completing Module 1: Safe

Module Sections	What Teachers Do	What Trainers Do
Overview **Your Own Need for Safety** **Pre-Training Assessment**	Read about safety concerns and how teachers keep children safe. Read and answer questions about the three examples of how teachers keep children safe and about their own need for safety. Complete the *Pre-Training Assessment* and list 3–5 skills to improve or topics to learn more about. Share responses and chart feedback.	Observe teachers and review ongoing notes. Discuss with teachers • responses to questions about the examples • personal safety experiences and how they relate to children's safety • the *Pre-Training Assessment* When possible, evaluate *Pre-Training Assessment* responses by observing.
Learning Activity A, Using Your Knowledge of Infants and Toddlers to Ensure Their Safety	Read about typical characteristics of infants and toddlers that are important to consider when ensuring their safety. Complete the chart showing how they use what they know about child development to keep infants and toddlers safe. Share responses and chart feedback. Continue adding examples to the child development chart while working on the module.	Discuss what teachers do to keep children safe. Review teachers' examples of what they do to ensure the safety of infants and toddlers. Encourage teachers to add examples to the development chart while working on the module.
Learning Activity B, Creating and Maintaining a Safe Environment	Read about ways teachers maintain safe indoor and outdoor spaces for infants and toddlers. Review the characteristics of a safe environment and think about their responsibility for ensuring children's safety. Create and use daily and monthly safety checklists to assess their indoor and outdoor environments, identify items that need attention, and take steps to improve safety. Discuss needed improvements with colleagues and trainer. Make and check off changes. With colleagues, develop a daily and monthly safety check schedule. Share responses and chart feedback.	Review checklists and help teachers identify potential dangers. Check to see that teachers are conducting safety checks every day. Help teachers plan ways to improve environmental safety. Confirm that teachers made environmental safety changes.

Completing Module 1: Safe (continued)

Module Sections	What Teachers Do	What Trainers Do
Learning Activity C, Preparing for and Handling Emergencies	Read about preparing for and responding to children's injuries and to emergencies. Review their program's emergency plan and answer questions about responding to injuries and emergencies. If necessary, review program emergency procedures with supervisor. Share responses and chart feedback.	Discuss answers to questions. Encourage teachers to review and practice emergency procedures on a regular basis. As needed, provide resources or referrals for additional first-aid and emergency-response training. When possible, observe emergency drills and provide feedback.
Learning Activity D, Introducing Safety Practices to Children	Read about modeling and talking about safety practices with infants and toddlers throughout the day. Observe children and a colleague during a routine or activity, and think about how to enhance safety. Share responses and chart feedback.	Observe teachers and provide feedback on how they model safety practices. Encourage teachers to review their program's guidelines for neighborhood walks. Help teachers develop a few simple safety rules to introduce to toddlers.
Reflecting on Your Learning	Review the chart begun in *Learning Activity A* and add examples. Review responses to the *Pre-Training Assessment,* summarize progress by responding to questions, and consider curriculum connections and partnerships with families. Share responses and chart feedback. Complete the knowledge and competency assessments.	Discuss teachers' additions to their child development charts and their progress summaries. Give and score the *Knowledge Assessment.* Schedule an observation to complete the *Competency Assessment* for the module. Provide feedback as teachers work on the assessments.

Strategies to Extend Learning

Have teachers kneel on the floor to view the environment from the children's perspective. Discuss safety precautions taken (e.g., using electrical outlet covers) as well as any unaddressed hazards teachers discover. Be sure to emphasize safety concerns that are especially important for infants and toddlers.

Distribute information about and encourage teachers to attend safety courses or workshops. Consider training offered by their program, by local organizations, or by national groups such as the American Red Cross.

Ask teachers to individualize the safety checklists. Checklists should correspond to their room arrangements, furnishings, materials, equipment, and outdoor areas.

Encourage teachers to keep records of how they address potentially dangerous items and conditions. This exercise will help teachers deepen their understanding that maintaining a safe environment is an ongoing part of their jobs.

Suggest that teachers obtain and share safety publications with families. Consider materials from organizations such as the American Academy of Pediatrics and the Consumer Product Safety Commission.

Ask local emergency service providers to offer training on how to respond during weather-related emergencies or other natural disasters that might occur in your area (e.g., lightning storms, tornadoes, and earthquakes). The local American Red Cross chapter and fire department can be excellent resources.

Completing Module 2: Healthy

Module Sections	What Teachers Do	What Trainers Do
Overview **Your Own Health and Nutrition** **Pre-Training Assessment**	Read about strategies that promote children's health. Read and answer questions about the three examples of how teachers support wellness and about their own health and nutrition. Complete the *Pre-Training Assessment* and list 3–5 skills to improve or topics to learn more about. Share responses and chart feedback.	Observe teachers and review ongoing notes. Discuss with teachers • responses to questions about the examples • personal health habits (if teachers want to share information) and how they relate to children's health • the *Pre-Training Assessment* When possible, evaluate *Pre-Training Assessment* responses by observing.
Learning Activity A, Using Your Knowledge of Infants and Toddlers to Promote Good Health and Nutrition	Read about typical characteristics of infants and toddlers that affect their health. Complete a chart to show how they use what they know about child development to promote children's health. Share responses and chart feedback. Continue adding examples to the child development chart while working on the module.	Discuss what teachers do to keep children healthy. Review and discuss the examples that teachers recorded on their development charts. Encourage teachers to add examples to their charts while working on the module.
Learning Activity B, Creating and Maintaining a Hygienic Environment	Read about creating and maintaining a hygienic environment and about following recommended health procedures. Use a "Hygienic Environment Checklist" and develop a plan for improving health practices. Set a date to review the checklist again. Share responses and chart feedback.	Review completed checklists and help teachers identify practices that need improvement. Agree on a date for a follow-up check. If possible, use the "Hygienic Environment Checklist" to assess each teacher's environment. Compare those evaluations with the teachers' assessments. Meet with teachers and colleagues to discuss improvement strategies that will promote wellness and reduce disease.

Completing Module 2: Healthy (continued)

Module Sections	What Teachers Do	What Trainers Do
Learning Activity C, Introducing Health and Nutrition to Infants and Toddlers	Read about how to introduce health and nutrition to infants and toddlers. Observe a colleague and children during a daily routine. Think about what the children might be learning about health and nutrition and how the colleague promoted good health habits. Share responses and chart feedback.	If possible, observe teachers during a caregiving routine and provide feedback on how they promote health and nutrition. Discuss with teachers how they model healthy practices throughout the day.
Learning Activity D, Recognizing and Reporting the Signs of Child Abuse and Neglect	Study definitions and signs of different types of child abuse and neglect. Read about picking up clues, possible abuse and neglect in early childhood programs, and reporting. Answer questions about recognizing and reporting possible child abuse and neglect. Review their program's procedures and state and local procedures for reporting abuse and neglect. Describe the procedures. Read reasons why teachers might be reluctant to report signs of possible neglect and abuse and explain why they must report. Share responses and chart feedback.	Provide definitions of and guidance on child abuse and neglect. Present information from the program and from state and local governments. Review answers to the questions and help teachers compare them to those provided in the *Answer Sheets*.
Reflecting on Your Learning	Review the chart begun in *Learning Activity A* and add examples. Review responses to the *Pre-Training Assessment*, summarize progress by responding to questions, and consider curriculum connections and partnerships with families. Share responses and chart feedback. Complete the knowledge and competency assessments.	Discuss teachers' additions to their child development charts and their progress summaries. Give and score the *Knowledge Assessment*. Schedule an observation to complete the *Competency Assessment* for the module. Provide feedback as teachers work on the assessments.

Strategies to Extend Learning

Ask teachers to review and practice their programs' procedures for handwashing, diapering, toileting, washing and disinfecting, and feeding and eating.

Introduce the USDA Child and Adult Care Food Program requirements for infant/toddler meals and snacks. Ask teachers to review menus for snacks and meals and to recommend changes, if necessary, to ensure that foods served to children meet USDA guidelines.

Encourage teachers to talk with families about continuity between their homes and the program for such things as introducing new foods, toilet learning, and dressing appropriately for the weather. Assist them in writing letters to families that explain how families and teachers can work together. (*The Creative Curriculum for Infants & Toddlers* includes sample letters that share ideas with families about daily routines.)

Serve healthy snacks at staff meetings and workshops. Discuss ways teachers model good nutrition and hygiene practices, such as healthy eating habits and washing their hands before eating.

Ask teachers to help you organize a collection of local resources on the prevention of child abuse and neglect. Work together to plan and implement family support activities at the program.

Encourage teachers to meet regularly to discuss stress that may affect children and families and to suggest strategies for offering assistance. Ask teachers to share their healthy approaches to stress, and encourage them to support each other on the job.

Research and share information about health issues relevant to a particular family or to the community in which you work. For example, lead and other types of environmental pollution are known problems in some communities, or a family might have a child with fetal alcohol syndrome or another health-related condition.

Completing Module 3: Learning Environment

Module Sections	What Teachers Do	What Trainers Do
Overview **Your Own Responses to the Environment** **Pre-Training Assessment**	Read about indoor and outdoor environments that support relationships and encourage exploration, and about daily routines and schedules. Read and answer questions about the three examples of how teachers create environments, routines, and schedules for infants and toddlers and about personal responses to the environment. Complete the *Pre-Training Assessment* and list 3–5 skills to improve or topics to learn more about. Share responses and chart feedback.	Observe teachers and environments and review ongoing notes. Discuss with teachers • responses to questions about the examples • personal experiences in different environments and how they relate to creating appropriate environments for infants and toddlers • the *Pre-Training Assessment* When possible, evaluate the *Pre-Training Assessment* responses by observing.
Learning Activity A, Using Your Knowledge of Infants and Toddlers to Create a Responsive and Supportive Environment	Read about typical characteristics of infants and toddlers that are important to consider when creating a learning environment for infants and toddlers. Complete the chart showing how they use what they know about child development to create a supportive environment. Share responses and feedback. Continue adding examples to the child development chart while working on the module.	Discuss how teachers create environments that support infant and toddler development. Review and discuss the examples that teachers recorded on their development charts. Encourage teachers to add examples to the chart while working on the module.
Learning Activity B, Creating and Maintaining the Caregiving Environment	Read about organizing separate areas for different routines and activities and to support each child's development. Complete the "Infant/Toddler Environment Checklist" and describe desirable changes to the environment. Identify two children with different characteristics and plan ways to support their exploration and learning. Share responses and chart feedback.	Review the teachers' checklists and discuss their plans to improve indoor and outdoor environments. If possible, meet with teachers and their colleagues to review proposed changes and to encourage teamwork. Encourage teachers regularly to observe children's responses to the environment and to determine when additional changes are needed.

Completing Module 3: Learning Environment (continued)

Module Sections	What Teachers Do	What Trainers Do
Learning Activity C, Selecting and Displaying Toys and Materials	Read about criteria for materials that are appropriate for infants and toddlers and about displaying them in ways that promote exploration and play. Evaluate classroom toys and materials to see whether they meet the criteria. Share responses and chart feedback.	Discuss the criteria for appropriate materials and help teachers decide whether their classroom materials meet the criteria. Encourage teachers to add or rotate toys in response to children's changing interests and growing skills.
Learning Activity D, Planning Daily Routines and a Flexible Schedule	Read about using daily routines to build relationships and about planning a flexible schedule to meet the needs of each child. Review and revise the daily schedule. Share responses and chart feedback.	Help teachers think about daily routines as opportunities to build relationships. If possible, observe a daily routine and encourage teachers to use the routine to support children's learning. Discuss the daily schedule. Encourage teachers to plan individual schedules for infants and consistent but flexible schedules for toddlers.
Reflecting on Your Learning	Review the chart begun in *Learning Activity A* and add examples. Review responses to the *Pre-Training Assessment*, summarize progress by answering questions, and consider curriculum connections and partnerships with families. Share responses and chart feedback. Complete the knowledge and competency assessments.	Discuss teachers' additions to their child development charts and their progress summaries. Give and score the *Knowledge Assessment*. Schedule an observation to complete the *Competency Assessment* for this module. Provide feedback as teachers work on the assessments.

Strategies to Extend Learning

Have teachers think about how their program environments convey the following messages to children:

- This is a good place to be.

- You belong here. You are a valued member of this community.

- This is a place you can trust.

- There are places you can be by yourself when you want to be.

- You can do many things on your own.

- This is a safe place to explore and try your ideas.

Then ask them to consider changes that will enhance the way the environment imparts these messages.

Have teachers make a wish list of materials they would like to add to their environments. Encourage them to review the "Some Good Toys and Materials for Infants and Toddlers" chart and to add ordinary, everyday materials to their classrooms.

Provide materials for making classroom labels, and help teachers organize and label storage containers and places. Use materials such as clear and colored adhesive paper, poster board, construction paper, permanent markers, and glue.

Suggest that teachers plan and hold a workshop for families on responsive environments at the program and at home. Discuss such topics as

- messages in the environment

- using everyday materials to support children's learning

- everyday routines as learning opportunities

Help teachers set up a system for collecting and storing useful materials. Teachers can use cardboard boxes and plastic containers to store dramatic play props, paper, art materials, and so on.

Completing Module 4: Physical

Module Sections	What Teachers Do	What Trainers Do
Overview **Taking Care of Your Body** **Pre-Training Assessment**	Read about fine and gross motor development and how teachers promote infants' and toddlers' physical development. Read and answer questions about the three examples of how teachers promote children's physical development and about staying physically fit, themselves. Complete the *Pre-Training Assessment* and list 3–5 skills to improve or topics to learn more about. Share responses and chart feedback.	Observe teachers and review ongoing notes. Discuss with teachers • responses to questions about the examples • ways to handle the physical demands of their jobs • the *Pre-Training Assessment* When possible, evaluate *Pre-Training Assessment* responses by observing.
Learning Activity A, Using Your Knowledge of Infants and Toddlers to Support Physical Development	Read about infants' and toddlers' typical physical development, how physical development is connected to other aspects of development, and physical development alerts. Complete the chart showing how teachers use what they know about infants and toddlers to support children's motor development. Share responses and chart feedback. Continue adding examples to the child development chart while working on the module.	Discuss what teachers do to encourage children to develop and use gross and fine motor skills. Review and discuss the examples that teachers recorded on their development charts. Encourage teachers to add examples to the chart while working on the module.
Learning Activity B, Creating an Environment That Supports Physical Development	Read about setting up and adapting environments to help children develop their fine and gross motor skills. Observe two children for three days and summarize each child's physical skills. Note how the environment supports physical development and how it can be enhanced to further promote children's physical development. Share responses and chart feedback.	Review teachers' observation notes and discuss changes teachers can make to the environment to encourage children's motor development. As appropriate, suggest equipment, materials, room arrangement strategies, and adaptations.

Completing Module 4: Physical (continued)

Module Sections	What Teachers Do	What Trainers Do
Learning Activity C, Responding as Infants and Toddlers Use Physical Skills	Read about how teachers' relationships with infants and toddlers support physical development and how to encourage infants' and toddlers' self-confidence. Read descriptions of infants and toddlers who are using physical skills in three example scenarios. Describe appropriate teacher responses. Select two children and describe their physical skills. Plan and try ways to support their use of physical skills. Record the children's reactions to the teacher's support and what the teacher learned from the experience. Share responses and chart feedback.	Discuss appropriate teacher responses to children's use of physical skills in the example scenarios. Review and discuss the charts teachers create about supporting the physical development of two children. Suggest materials, routines, and activities that give children opportunities to practice and refine motor skills.
Learning Activity D, Supporting Physical Development Throughout the Day	Read about supporting the development of physical skills while children are involved in daily routines and while playing. Describe a routine or play experience during which they supported physical development. Consider the experience through the eyes of the child and from the teacher's perspective. Think about how to continue to support development of fine and gross motor skills. Share responses and chart feedback.	Discuss how teachers supported physical development during diapering, eating, or dressing. Help teachers discover ways to continue supporting physical development throughout the day. If possible, observe teachers during a routine and provide feedback about the ways they support children's physical development.
Reflecting on Your Learning	Review the chart begun in *Learning Activity A* and add examples. Review responses to the *Pre-Training Assessment*, summarize progress by answering questions, and consider curriculum connections and partnerships with families. Share responses and chart feedback. Complete the knowledge and competency assessments.	Discuss teachers' additions to their physical development charts and their progress summaries. Give and score the *Knowledge Assessment*. Schedule an observation to complete the *Competency Assessment* for this module. Provide feedback as the assessments are undertaken.

Strategies to Extend Learning

Observe children who seem to have unusual delays in fine or gross motor skill development. Share your observation notes with teachers and, if needed, with the children's families. Encourage families to follow up with their pediatrician or a specialist, if necessary.

Hold a workshop during which teachers use their fine motor skills for finger painting, completing puzzles, building with Duplos®, stringing beads, and playing with water. Point out the small muscle skills developed through these and similar activities.

Lead role playing for teachers to practice encouraging children to use physical skills. Teachers can practice offering cues and challenges to help children develop and refine their skills. Ask two teachers to pretend that they are children engaged in an activity, while a third teacher provides encouragement, cues, and challenges. Switch roles so everyone has a turn playing a child and the teacher. Discuss how it feels to give and receive encouragement.

Completing Module 5: Cognitive

Module Sections	What Teachers Do	What Trainers Do
Overview **Your Own Experiences as a Learner** **Pre-Training Assessment**	Read about cognitive development and how teachers promote children's thinking skills. Read and answer questions about the three examples of how teachers promote cognitive development and about a personal learning experience. Complete the *Pre-Training Assessment* and list 3–5 skills to improve or topics to learn more about. Share responses and chart feedback.	Observe teachers and review ongoing notes. Discuss with teachers • responses to questions about the examples • personal learning experiences and how those experiences apply to caring for infants and toddlers • the *Pre-Training Assessment* When possible, evaluate *Pre-Training Assessment* responses by observing.
Learning Activity A, Using Your Knowledge of Infants and Toddlers to Support Cognitive Development	Read about how infants and toddlers think and learn, how cognitive development is connected to other aspects of development, and cognitive development alerts. Complete the chart showing how teachers use what they know about infants and toddlers to promote cognitive development. Share responses and chart feedback. Continue adding examples to the child development chart while working on the module.	Discuss what teachers do to promote infants' and toddlers' cognitive development. Review and discuss the examples that teachers recorded on their development charts. Encourage teachers to add examples to the chart while working on the module. Provide materials for making toys.
Learning Activity B, Creating an Environment That Encourages Exploration and Discovery	Read about environments that enable infants and toddlers to explore and gain new skills, and about selecting and making toys that support cognitive development. Make a toy, introduce it to a child, report what happened, and share directions with colleagues and families. Share responses and chart feedback.	Discuss how the teacher-made toys support cognitive development. Encourage teachers to share their toy-making directions and plans with colleagues and families.

Completing Module 5: Cognitive (continued)

Module Sections	What Teachers Do	What Trainers Do
Learning Activity C, Supporting Infants' and Toddlers' Thinking Skills During Routines	Read about how relationships support cognitive development and how to use routines to encourage exploration and discovery. Observe a colleague during a routine and list five things teachers can do during the routine to support children's thinking skills. Share responses and chart feedback.	Discuss how teachers use routines to support cognitive development. Review examples of ways to support thinking skills, and assist teachers in finding additional ways.
Learning Activity D, Encouraging Cognitive Development Throughout the Day	Read about when and how to guide children's play and how to plan simple activities that correspond to children's interests and skills. Plan and carry out an activity. Review how well the activity followed activity guidelines. Share responses and chart feedback.	Review the activity guidelines with teachers. If possible, observe the planned activities. Help teachers think about what went well and what they would like to change.
Reflecting on Your Learning	Review the chart begun in *Learning Activity A* and add examples. Review responses to the *Pre-Training Assessment*, summarize progress by responding to questions, and consider curriculum connections and partnerships with families. Share responses and chart feedback. Complete the knowledge and competency assessments.	Discuss teachers' additions to their cognitive development charts and their progress summaries. Give and score the *Knowledge Assessment*. Schedule an observation to complete the *Competency Assessment* for the module. Provide feedback as teachers work on the assessments.

Strategies to Extend Learning

Plan a toy-making workshop. Encourage teachers to share their ideas for making toys and describe what children learn when they use them. Have teachers play roles, pretending to use the toy with an infant or toddler. Invite families to attend and help make the toys.

Conduct a workshop on the theory and research that inform early childhood education. Help teachers learn about recent brain research and about the work of Jean Piaget, Lev Vygotsky, Howard Gardner, and Sara Smilansky. Have teachers discuss implications for practice.

Have teachers list open-ended questions to ask older toddlers. They should include questions that would encourage toddlers to describe what they are doing, recall past experiences, remember someone who is not present, make predictions, and solve simple problems. Have them use the list to think about which the types of questions they ask frequently.

Completing Module 6: Communication

Module Sections	What Teachers Do	What Trainers Do
Overview **Your Own Experiences With Communication** **Pre-Training Assessment**	Read about communication and language skills and how teachers promote them. Read and respond to questions about the three examples of how teachers promote children's communication skills and about personal communication skills. Complete the *Pre-Training Assessment* and list 3–5 skills to improve or topics to learn more about. Share responses and chart feedback.	Observe teachers and review ongoing notes. Discuss with teachers • responses to questions about the examples • teachers' memories of their early language and literacy experiences, and how those experiences relate to promoting children's communication skills • the *Pre-Training Assessment* When possible, evaluate *Pre-Training Assessment* responses by observing.
Learning Activity A, Using Your Knowledge of Infants and Toddlers to Promote Communication Skills	Read about how infants and toddlers develop language and literacy skills, typical developmental characteristics that are related to language development, how language development is connected to other aspects of development, and language and communication development alerts. Complete the chart showing how teachers use what they know about infants and toddlers to promote communication skills. Share responses and chart feedback. Continue adding examples to the child development chart while working on the module.	Discuss what teachers do to help children develop and use language skills. Review and discuss the examples teachers recorded on their development charts. Encourage teachers to add examples to the chart while working on the module.
Learning Activity B, Creating an Environment That Invites Infants and Toddlers to Enjoy Sounds, Language, Pictures, and Print	Read about how the environment can encourage communication and support emerging literacy exploration. Describe how their environment currently encourages language skills and literacy learning, and note ways to improve practices. Share responses and chart feedback.	Review charts and suggest ways to make changes to enhance language and literacy environments.

Completing Module 6: Communication (continued)

Module Sections	What Teachers Do	What Trainers Do
Learning Activity C, Encouraging the Language Development of Infants and Toddlers	Read about how teachers encourage the language development of infants and toddlers. Take notes for three days on what they say and do to encourage the language development of two children. Use notes to answer questions about the children's experiences. Share responses and chart feedback.	Review and discuss teachers' notes and their strategies for encouraging language development. Offer feedback and suggestions.
Learning Activity D, Sharing Books With Infants and Toddlers	Read about the importance of reading aloud with children, choosing appropriate books, and strategies for reading aloud. Select two books that are appropriate for the children in their classroom. Read one to an individual child and one to a small group. Report each experience. Share responses and chart feedback.	Encourage teachers to assess the books in their classroom to make sure they are appropriate for young infants, mobile infants, or toddlers. Discuss teachers' reports about reading to one child and a small group. Help teachers compare the two experiences and discuss strategies for engaging children with books. Encourage teachers to keep track of when they read to individuals, to make sure every child has regular one-on-one reading experiences.
Reflecting on Your Learning	Review the chart begun in *Learning Activity A* and add examples. Review responses to the *Pre-Training Assessment*, summarize progress by answering questions, and consider curriculum connections and partnerships with families. Share responses and chart feedback. Complete the knowledge and competency assessments.	Discuss teachers' additions to their communication development charts and their progress summaries. Give and score the *Knowledge Assessment*. Schedule an observation to complete the *Competency Assessment* for the module. Provide feedback as the assessments are undertaken.

Strategies to Extend Learning

Invite a speech and language specialist to co-lead a workshop on early language development and signs of possible speech or language delays or disabilities. Work with the program director to establish a system for informing families of teachers' observations and making referrals to speech and language specialists, if necessary.

During classroom visits, model effective oral reading techniques. Begin by reading to children, individually or in small groups.

Help teachers set up a lending library so families may borrow books to read to their children at home. Encourage teachers to choose books according to the characteristics discussed in the module.

Work with teachers to plan a family workshop on what parents can do during the first five years to help their children become good readers and writers. You may want to use *Reading Right From the Start* as a resource.

Invite a children's librarian to visit the program to share information about books and library services for children and families.

Completing Module 7: Creative

Module Sections	What Teachers Do	What Trainers Do
Overview **Your Own Creativity** **Pre-Training Assessment**	Read about children's creativity and ways teachers support its development. Read and answer questions about the three examples of how teachers encourage children's creativity and about adult creativity. Complete the *Pre-Training Assessment* and list 3–5 skills to improve or topics to learn more about. Share responses and chart feedback.	Observe teachers and review ongoing notes. Discuss with teachers • responses to questions about the examples • teachers' exploration of open-ended materials • the *Pre-Training Assessment* When possible, evaluate *Pre-Training Assessment* responses by observing.
Learning Activity A, Using Your Knowledge of Infants and Toddlers to Encourage Creativity	Read about key characteristics and typical behaviors of infants and toddlers that are related to creativity. Begin a log of when children display key creative characteristics. Share examples of children's creative explorations with families and record some of the families' responses. Share responses and chart feedback.	Discuss what teachers do to promote children's creativity. Review and discuss the examples teachers recorded on their logs. Suggest additional ways teachers' interactions can support children's creativity and ways to communicate with families about their children's creativity.
Learning Activity B, Supporting Creativity Through Positive Interactions	Read about the importance of teachers' interactions with children and ways teachers encourage creativity throughout the day. Rate how well their environments and teaching practices support children's creativity throughout the day and identify any needed changes. Share responses and chart feedback.	Review and discuss teachers' examples and ratings. Observe teachers and discuss specific examples of how their interactions with children and other aspects of their environments encourage creativity.

Completing Module 7: Creative (continued)

Module Sections	What Teachers Do	What Trainers Do
Learning Activity C, Encouraging Creative Expression Though Music and Movement	Read about providing opportunities for children to listen to a variety of sounds and music, singing with children, encouraging creative movement, and playing rhythm instruments. Plan and implement a music and movement activity for one or several children. Think about what the children did and how the teacher responded. Share responses and chart feedback.	Review and discuss the music and movement activities that teachers planned and implemented, and their reports of what happened. Encourage teachers to work with colleagues to implement other new ideas for encouraging self-expression through music and movement.
Learning Activity D, Nurturing Creativity Through Art Experiences	Read about a variety of materials and activities that encourage children's exploration. Consider the implications of children's individual and developmental characteristics as activities are implemented. Review procedures and recipes for a few basic art experiences. Observe a child exploring art materials over a 3-day period. Use what they learn about the child to select, plan, and implement a new art activity to match the child's interests and skill level. Report what happened. Share responses and chart feedback.	Help teachers plan ways to provide a variety of open-ended art materials and experiences that allow children to begin exploring creative processes. Review and discuss observation notes and activity plans. If possible, observe teachers implementing the activities. Help clean up after messy activities. Model ways to include older children in cleanup: sweeping, wiping tables, putting creations in an undisturbed place, placing materials back on the shelf, and so on.
Reflecting on Your Learning	Review the log that was started in *Learning Activity A* and add more examples. Review responses to the *Pre-Training Assessment*, summarize progress by answering questions, and consider curriculum connections and partnerships with families. Share responses and chart feedback. Complete the knowledge and competency assessments.	Discuss teachers' additions to their logs and their progress summaries. Give and score the *Knowledge Assessment*. Schedule an observation to complete the *Competency Assessment* for this module. Provide feedback as the assessments are undertaken.

Strategies to Extend Learning

Offer a hands-on, open-ended workshop on the creative process. (For ideas, see *Learning to Play Again: A Constructivist Workshop for Adults* at http://www.journal.naeyc.org/btj/200305/ConstructWorkshops_Chalufour.pdf) Provide a wide variety of materials and encourage teachers to become fully involved. Help teachers focus on the process rather than the product of their creative effort. At the end of the workshop, ask participants to discuss their thoughts about focusing on the creative process. Discuss how their experiences will affect their approach to encouraging children's creativity.

Encourage teachers to identify what they really love to do and plan ways to explore their creativity in those areas. Have them think of ways to include their interests as they work with children.

Ask teachers to recall a time during their childhood when an adult supported their creativity. Guide them by asking questions such as, *What were you doing? What did the adult do and say? How did you feel?* Ask them to list the strategies adults used to encourage them. Next, ask teachers to think of a time when an adult prevented them from being creative. List the adult actions that interfered with their creativity. Use the two lists to discuss how teachers actively encourage children's creative efforts.

Have teachers set up a system for keeping examples of children's creativity in individual portfolios. Each portfolio can include photographs of children engaged in play and exploration, paintings and drawings, photographs of block structures or playdough creations, audiotaped music, descriptions of dance and movement activities, and so on. Both teachers and families can write brief notes describing children's creative explorations. Remind teachers to review the portfolios periodically and to share them with older children and their families.

Completing Module 8: Self

Module Sections	What Teachers Do	What Trainers Do
Overview **Your Own Sense of Self** **Pre-Training Assessment**	Read about how children develop a sense of self and the important roles that teachers and families play. Read and answer questions about the three examples of how teachers help children develop a sense of self and about their own experiences. Complete the *Pre-Training Assessment* and list 3–5 skills to improve or topics to learn more about. Share responses and chart feedback.	Observe teachers and review ongoing notes. Discuss with teachers • responses to questions about the examples • experiences that contributed to their values, expectations, and sense of identity and how their sense of self influences their relationships with children • the *Pre-Training Assessment* When possible, evaluate *Pre-Training Assessment* responses by observing.
Learning Activity A, Using Your Knowledge of Infants and Toddlers to Foster a Sense of Self	Read about the typical developmental characteristics of infants and toddlers that are related to developing a sense of self and the ways in which building a sense of self is connected to all aspects of development. Complete the chart showing how teachers use what they know about infants and toddlers to foster children's sense of self. Share responses and chart feedback. Continue adding examples to the child development chart while working on the module.	Discuss what teachers do to help children learn about themselves and others. Review and discuss the examples that teachers record on their development charts. Encourage teachers to add examples to the chart while working on the module.

Completing Module 8: Self (continued)

Module Sections	What Teachers Do	What Trainers Do
Learning Activity B, Offering a Program That Promotes Success	Read about strategies for getting to know individual children and about how teachers promote children's success through the environment, routines, activities, and interactions. Observe two children at different times of day. Use notes to plan ways to promote each child's success through interactions, the environment, activities, and routines. Share responses and chart feedback.	If possible, observe the same children that teachers observed. Help teachers assess interactions, the environment, activities, and routines to determine how well they contribute to children's positive sense of self. Discuss teachers' strategies and why they were or were not successful. Encourage teachers to work with colleagues to create a system for conducting regular observations of children and continually to evaluate their interactions with children. Stress that it is important to observe children regularly because children's abilities and interests change frequently.
Learning Activity C, Helping Children and Families Cope With Separation	Read about when and why infants and toddlers have difficulty handling separations and reunions, and how to help children and families cope with being apart. Think about a child who has strong feelings about separation. Describe what they do now to support the child and family during separation, and give examples of what else they could do. Share responses and chart feedback.	Review and discuss the teachers' examples of how they help children and families cope with separation. Help teachers think about why children and families have strong feelings about separation and about what else they can do to assist. If possible, observe teachers and provide feedback about how they help infants, toddlers, and their families cope with separation.
Learning Activity D, Supporting Toddlers During Toilet Learning	Read about how to recognize when a child is ready, willing, and able to start toilet learning; typical toddler characteristics that affect toilet learning; and how to work with families on toilet learning. Select a child who shows signs of being ready for toilet learning. Answer questions about supporting the child's toilet learning. Implement a plan and describe what happened. Share responses and chart feedback.	Review the signs that a toddler might be ready for toilet learning. Remind teachers that accidents are a normal part of toilet learning. If possible, observe the selected children. Discuss the readiness signs you observed and the teachers' plans to work on toilet learning with the children and their families. If possible, observe teachers during children's toileting and offer suggestions to help them support the children.

Completing Module 8: Self (continued)

Module Sections	What Teachers Do	What Trainers Do
Reflecting on Your Learning	Review the chart begun in *Learning Activity A* and add examples. Review responses to the *Pre-Training Assessment*, summarize progress by answering questions, and consider curriculum connections and partnerships with families. Share responses and chart feedback. Complete the knowledge and competency assessments.	Discuss teachers' additions to their child development charts and their progress summaries. Give and score the *Knowledge Assessment*. Schedule an observation to complete the *Competency Assessment* for the module. Provide feedback as the assessments are undertaken.

Strategies to Extend Learning

Have teachers think about people they especially enjoyed being with when they were children. Ask them to remember talking with one of those people. Ask questions, such as the following, to discuss how adults help children recognize their abilities and feel competent.

> *What did this person do or say to help you feel good about yourself?*
>
> *How did you feel about yourself at the time?*
>
> *How did your experiences with this person affect your sense of competence?*
>
> *What can you do and say to help children feel confident about their abilities?*

Encourage teachers to keep families updated about their children's skills, interests, and accomplishments. Have teachers role-play conversations with families about different ways to promote children's sense of competence through simple routines and activities at home.

Collect children's books and adult resources about toilet learning and separation. Have teachers review the books, discuss what they learned, and consider how they can use the books in their program.

Conduct a workshop on separations and reunions. To begin the workshop, have teachers imagine that they are at the airport, greeting or saying goodbye to loved ones. After they do so, have teachers brainstorm ways to make hellos and goodbyes smooth for the children and families in their groups.

Completing Module 9: Social

Module Sections	What Teachers Do	What Trainers Do
Overview **Your Own Social Development** **Pre-Training Assessment**	Read about the importance of social development and about how teachers promote children's social skills. Read and respond to questions about the three examples of how teachers promote children's social development and about adult social skills. Complete the *Pre-Training Assessment* and list 3–5 skills to improve or topics to learn more about. Share responses and chart feedback.	Observe teachers and review ongoing notes. Discuss with teachers • responses to questions about the examples • how infants and toddlers learn from teachers and how teachers model social skills • the *Pre-Training Assessment* When possible, evaluate *Pre-Training Assessment* responses by observing.
Learning Activity A, Using Your Knowledge of Infants and Toddlers to Promote Social Development	Read about how infants and toddlers develop social skills, typical characteristics of infants and toddlers related to social development, how social development is connected to other aspects of development, and social development alerts. Complete the chart showing how teachers use their knowledge of infants and toddlers to promote social development. Share responses and chart feedback. Continue adding examples to the child development chart while working on the module.	Discuss the teacher's role in helping infants and toddlers develop and use social skills. Review and discuss the examples teachers recorded on their charts. Encourage teachers to add examples to their charts while working on the module.
Learning Activity B, Creating an Environment That Supports Social Development	Read about how responsive interactions and the physical environment support infants' and toddlers' social development, and how to create a homelike setting. Read and think about environmental characteristics that support social development. Describe how one aspect of their environment currently supports social development. Plan and implement a change to the environment and report what happens. Share responses and chart feedback.	Discuss program features that support social development. Ask teachers to give examples of how their practices support social development. Review and offer feedback on plans and reports. If possible, observe in classrooms and offer appropriate suggestions.

Completing Module 9: Social (continued)

Module Sections	What Teachers Do	What Trainers Do
Learning Activity C, Helping Infants and Toddlers Learn to Care About Others	Read about recognizing and encouraging children's caring behavior. Conduct 5-minute observations, several times a day, for three days. Review notes and list examples of children's caring behavior. Think about the ways they model and encourage caring behavior. Make up and read a story to children about caring behavior. Describe children's responses. Share responses and chart feedback.	Discuss the idea that caring behaviors are learned over time and that infants and toddlers learn caring behaviors by watching and interacting with the adults who care for them. Review observation summaries and discuss ways to further encourage caring behaviors. Review and discuss the teachers' stories about caring behavior. If possible, observe when the teachers read the stories to children. Encourage teachers to continue making books about the children in their care.
Learning Activity D, Supporting Children's Play	Read about the importance of play, how to engage infants and toddlers through play, and encouraging pretend play. Conduct several observations of two children over a 3-day period. Describe the play, social skills being developed, and what the teacher did to support play. Share responses and chart feedback.	If possible, conduct classroom observations in order to learn about individual children and to assist teachers in identifying strategies to engage infants and toddlers through play. Review and discuss teachers' observation notes and reports.
Reflecting on Your Learning	Review the chart begun in *Learning Activity A* and add examples. Review the *Pre-Training Assessment*, summarize progress by answering questions, and consider curriculum connections and partnerships with families. Share responses and chart feedback. Complete the knowledge and competency assessments.	Discuss teachers' additions to their social development charts and their progress summaries. Give and score the *Knowledge Assessment*. Schedule an observation to complete the *Competency Assessment* for the module. Provide feedback as the assessments are undertaken.

Strategies to Extend Learning

Suggest that teachers ask a children's librarian to recommend children's books about caring behavior. Teachers can read and talk about them with individual children or with a small group of toddlers.

With a teacher, conduct several co-observations of children playing. Meet with the teacher to discuss what you saw and heard. Identify how children's social skills are related to development in other domains.

Encourage teachers to continue to observe children's caring behaviors. Arrange for teachers to use a digital camera and printer. Have teachers photograph children who are behaving in caring ways. Encourage them to use the photos to illustrate stories about what the children were doing and to share the stories with the children.

Hold a workshop about imitating and pretending. Discuss the kinds of toys, dress-up clothes, and other props that encourage pretend play. Have teachers evaluate their classroom materials and list items that they could add to support pretend play. Suggest ideas for simple prop boxes and have teachers make them.

Completing Module 10: Guidance

Module Sections	What Teachers Do	What Trainers Do
Overview **Your Own Self-Discipline** **Pre-Training Assessment**	Read about self-control and how responsive relationships and positive guidance strategies help infants and toddlers learn acceptable behavior. Read and respond to questions about the three examples of how teachers guide children's behavior and about how self-discipline guides their own behavior at work and home. Complete the *Pre-Training Assessment* and list 3–5 skills to improve or topics to learn more about. Share responses and chart feedback.	Observe teachers and review ongoing notes. Discuss with teachers • responses to questions about the examples • self-disciplinary experiences and how their experiences relate to helping children develop self-control • the *Pre-Training Assessment* When possible, evaluate *Pre-Training Assessment* responses by observing.
Learning Activity A, Using Your Knowledge of Infants and Toddlers to Guide Their Behavior	Read about typical behavioral characteristics of infants and toddlers and how to offer a program that prevents or minimizes unwanted behaviors. Complete a chart to show how they use their knowledge of child development to guide children's behavior. Share responses and chart feedback. Continue adding examples to the chart while working on the module.	Discuss how teachers design their programs to minimize unacceptable behavior and encourage desirable behavior. Review and discuss the examples that teachers recorded on their charts. Encourage teachers to add examples to the chart while working on the module.
Learning Activity B, Understanding and Responding to Children's Temperaments	Read about several aspects of temperament that affect the behavior of infants and toddlers. Answer questions about their own temperament. Choose a child and take notes on what the child does during routines and activities over a 3-day period. Answer questions about the child's temperament and their own, and about using what they learned to provide positive guidance. Share responses and chart feedback.	Check teachers' understanding of the traits discussed in the module. Emphasize that behaviors related to each trait range along a continuum. Review teachers' observation notes and discuss ways to use their understanding of the child's temperament to offer positive guidance.

Completing Module 10: Guidance (continued)

Module Sections	What Teachers Do	What Trainers Do
Learning Activity C, Using a Positive Guidance Approach	Read about using a variety of positive guidance strategies and how to choose strategies that fit the child and the situation. Take notes on a child's behavior over a 3-day period. Think about possible reasons for the behavior and choose appropriate guidance strategies. Share responses and chart feedback.	If possible, observe each teacher. Discuss the guidance strategies you observed and how they were chosen to fit the child and the situation. Review observation notes and comment on the guidance strategies selected.
Learning Activity D, Preventing and Responding to Problem Behavior	Read about common behavioral problems of infants and toddlers, probable causes, and the importance of working together with families. Focus on a child whose behavior presents ongoing problems. Describe the behavior and how teachers usually respond. Work with the child's family to develop a joint plan for responding to the behavior at home and at the program. Implement the plan and evaluate the results. Share responses and chart feedback.	If possible, observe children with problem behavior and share notes and perceptions with their teachers. If asked, help teachers prepare for the discussions with the children's families. Help teachers implement classroom strategies for responding to the behavior. Consult regularly to discuss the children's progress. Emphasize continued use of positive guidance to respond to problem behavior.
Reflecting on Your Learning	Review the chart begun in *Learning Activity A* and add examples. Review responses to the *Pre-Training Assessment*, summarize progress by responding to questions, and consider curriculum connections and partnerships with families. Share responses and chart feedback. Complete the knowledge and competency assessments.	Discuss teachers' additions to their child development charts and their progress summaries. Give and score the *Knowledge Assessment*. Schedule an observation to complete the *Competency Assessment* for the module. Provide feedback as the assessments are undertaken.

Strategies to Extend Learning

Use the information in this module and others to make a large chart that summarizes the development of infants and toddlers. Post the chart where all teachers can see it. Next to the chart, post a piece of paper with the question, *How can you use this information to support the development of self-control?* Ask teachers to write their suggestions and discuss their ideas at a staff meeting.

Sponsor a workshop for parents and teachers to discuss typical behaviors of infants and toddlers, what causes them, and appropriate guidance strategies to use at home and at the program. Help teachers plan the agenda and select key ideas to share with parents.

Encourage teachers to meet regularly to discuss children whose behavior is problematic. Identify possible causes of their behavior and plan strategies for helping children learn acceptable ways to behave. Remind teachers to maintain the confidentiality of information about children and families.

Offer to audio- or videotape teachers' conversations and interactions with children. Review the tape together and note the language and strategies teachers used to guide children's behavior.

Work with teachers and families to observe children whose behavior interferes with full participation in program activities. Help the teachers and families to plan ways to help the children learn alternative behaviors at home and at the program. If this approach is not effective, help the teachers and families work with early childhood mental health specialists.

Completing Module 11: Families

Module Sections	What Teachers Do	What Trainers Do
Overview **Your Own Views About Families** **Pre-Training Assessment**	Read about the importance of partnerships with families, how teachers and families contribute to positive relationships, and how partnerships are built. Read and answer questions about the three examples of how teachers work with families, about their childhood experiences, and about their current views. Complete the *Pre-Training Assessment* and list 3–5 skills to improve or topics to learn more about. Share responses and chart feedback.	Observe teachers and review ongoing notes. Discuss with teachers • responses to questions about the examples • teachers' family experiences and how their views and pressures on families affect their work • the *Pre-Training Assessment* When possible, evaluate *Pre-Training Assessment* responses by observing.
Learning Activity A, Building Partnerships With Families	Read about the benefits of partnerships, types of information that families and teachers can share, ways to learn about families, and multiple ways to communicate with families. Select a family they want to know better, select and try an approach, and describe what they learned and how they used their understanding to build a partnership. Share responses and chart feedback.	Observe interactions between teachers and family members. Give objective descriptions of their verbal and nonverbal communication. Discuss what teachers learned about the families and how they were able to strengthen partnerships. Suggest ways of strengthening partnerships with other families. Discuss teachers' communication strategies, such as their use of newsletters, family journals, bulletin boards, and telephone calls.
Learning Activity B, Resolving Differences	Read about when to address differences with families and how to address them in positive ways. Describe a time they had a difference of opinion or misunderstanding with a family and how they handled it. Consider how they might handle a future difference of opinion or misunderstanding. Share responses and chart feedback.	Review the effectiveness of teachers' strategies and suggest improvements, if necessary. Suggest additional ways to handle differences of opinion and misunderstandings.

Completing Module 11: Families (continued)

Module Sections	What Teachers Do	What Trainers Do
Learning Activity C, Offering Ways for Families to Be Involved	Read about a variety of ways to welcome families and involve them in the program. Select a new family-involvement strategy, implement it, and report results. Share responses and chart feedback.	Encourage teachers to ask families how they would like to be involved. Discuss the families' responses. Review family-involvement strategies and provide encouragement and suggestions. Offer to help get supplies, if necessary. Help teachers set realistic expectations for family involvement.
Learning Activity D, Planning and Holding Conferences With Families	Read about the goals of holding conferences with families, and how to plan and conduct them. Schedule a conference with a family. Prepare for the conference by organizing the child's portfolio, summarizing the child's developmental progress, and thinking about future steps. Conduct and evaluate the conference. Share responses and chart feedback.	Discuss the importance of holding regular conferences to review each child's development thoroughly. Help teachers prepare for conferences by discussing their planning forms. Help teachers conduct a practice conference. If possible, attend conferences. Offer feedback on tone, body language, shared information, and the overall effectiveness of the conference. Discuss teachers' feelings about the conferences.
Learning Activity E, Providing Support to Families	Read about sharing information with families about typical child growth and development, helping families locate resources, helping them deal with separations and reunions, and recognizing when families are under stress. Think about times during a two-week period when they offer support to families. Report the support they extended, the families' responses, and the outcomes. Share responses and chart feedback.	Review the teachers' reports about reaching out to families, discuss their experiences, and answer questions about supporting families. Emphasize the importance of following program policies with regard to confidentiality and referrals. Discuss signs of children's stress. Discuss guidelines for talking about situations with a supervisor and referring a family to a professional.

Completing Module 11: Families (continued)

Module Sections	What Teachers Do	What Trainers Do
Reflecting on Your Learning	Review responses to the *Pre-Training Assessment*, summarize progress by answering questions, and consider curriculum connections and partnerships with families. Share responses and chart feedback. Complete the knowledge and competency assessments.	Discuss teachers' progress summaries. Give and score the *Knowledge Assessment*. Schedule an observation to complete the *Competency Assessment* for the module. Provide feedback as the assessments are undertaken.

Strategies to Extend Learning

Lead a discussion about the similarities and differences between the families teachers that grew up in and today's families. Provide current statistics about families, e.g., single-parent families, families with two working spouses, those with children from previous marriages, and families who live far away from their own parents and siblings.

Provide information about signs of significant family stress. Invite appropriate agencies to give presentations about responding when a family member appears to need immediate support. Develop a list of public and private, community and state organizations that provide services to families (e.g., hotlines and support groups). Review program policies and procedures for referring families.

Work with community leaders to offer a workshop for teachers on diversity. Discuss the cultures of the program's families and ways to provide a program that values and responds to diversity.

Help teachers conduct an informal family survey. Identify the kinds of information that they would like to receive from the program and in what form (e.g., newsletters, informal chats, message centers, phone calls, or bulletin boards).

Completing Module 12: Program Management

Module Sections	What Teachers Do	What Trainers Do
Overview **Managing Your Own Life** **Pre-Training Assessment**	Read about the managerial skills teachers use to plan, conduct, and evaluate their programs and why individualizing the program is an important managerial responsibility. Read and respond to questions about the three examples of how teachers effectively manage a program and about how they manage their own lives. Complete the *Pre-Training Assessment* and list 3–5 skills to improve or topics to learn more about. Share responses and chart feedback.	Observe teachers and review ongoing notes. Discuss with teachers • responses to questions about the examples • their managerial experiences and challenges • the *Pre-Training Assessment* When possible, evaluate *Pre-Training Assessment* responses by observing.
Learning Activity A, Getting to Know Each Child	Read about the importance of conducting observations and about guidelines for ongoing, systematic, and complete observations. Analyze examples of observation notes that are objective and accurate and notes that are not. Observe a child for 5–10 minutes each day for a week and take notes. At least twice during the week, conduct a joint observation and compare notes. Analyze the notes to be sure they are objective, accurate, and complete. Share responses and chart feedback.	Make sure teachers understand that observation is a critical skill for early childhood professionals. Teachers will use observation skills while completing the modules and throughout their early childhood careers. If possible, conduct and discuss at least two co-observations of the child. Especially when this is not possible, make sure teachers conduct joint observations with colleagues or supervisors. Discuss examples of accurate and objective notes that avoid the use of labels. Provide support and assistance if teachers need to repeat the activity.

Completing Module 12: Program Management (continued)

Module Sections	What Teachers Do	What Trainers Do
Learning Activity B, Organizing and Using Portfolios	Read about creating portfolios that document infants' and toddlers' growth and development, the kinds of items to include, how to store portfolios, and how to share them with children and families. During a 2-week period, collect items to include in a portfolio for the child observed in *Learning Activity A*. Explain how each item documents the child's development. Develop and describe a system for organizing and storing the portfolio. Share responses and chart feedback.	Explain why portfolios are an effective way to track progress and plan individualized programs. Review the portfolio descriptions and suggest additional items to include. Suggest ways to involve families in selecting items to include in portfolios. Discuss the contents, organization, and use of the portfolios that the teachers compile.
Learning Activity C, Responding to Each Child's Needs and Interests	Read about what it means to individualize the program, strategies for individualizing different elements of the program, and meeting the needs of children with disabilities. Select the same child from *Learning Activities A* and *B* and summarize what they learned. Plan ways to meet the child's individual needs and build on the child's strengths, skills, and interests. Share responses and chart feedback.	Help teachers analyze their observations and portfolios and what they learned about the children's strengths, interests, and needs. Review and discuss ways to meet each child's individual needs and build on each child's interests. Encourage teachers to establish a system for observing all of the children regularly. If a child with disabilities is enrolled, discuss ways to become knowledgeable about the child, the family, and the specific disability.
Learning Activity D, Working as a Team to Plan and Evaluate the Program	Read about daily, weekly, and long-range planning; evaluating the program; and changing plans on the basis of evaluation information. As a team, review information about the children in their group. Develop, implement, and evaluate a weekly plan. Share responses and chart feedback.	Review and provide feedback on weekly plans. If appropriate, attend planning and evaluation meetings with teachers and their colleagues. Help teachers assess the effectiveness of the format and approach they now use for weekly planning. If changes are needed, offer to assist.

Completing Module 12: Program Management (continued)

Module Sections	What Teachers Do	What Trainers Do
Reflecting on Your Learning	Review responses to the *Pre-Training Assessment*, summarize progress by answering questions, and consider curriculum connections and partnerships with families. Share responses and chart feedback. Complete the knowledge and competency assessments.	Discuss teachers' progress summaries. Give and score the *Knowledge Assessment*. Schedule an observation to complete the *Competency Assessment* for the module. Provide feedback as the assessments are undertaken.

Strategies to Extend Learning

Introduce a variety of observation and documentation formats. Include formats such as anecdotal recordkeeping, time sampling, event sampling, rating scales, and skills checklists. Encourage teachers to pick the instruments or formats that best serve particular needs, such as assessing children's developmental levels, evaluating the environment, documenting children's progress in a specific area, or keeping records to discuss with families.

Provide a video camera and tripod that teachers may use indoors or outdoors. Encourage them to let the camera run, cinema verité style. Together, view what the camera recorded. Discuss what the children did, materials and skills they used, how they interacted with each other and with teachers, and how the teachers responded. Help teachers identify their teaching and caregiving styles; different methods used for different purposes and with different children; and the ways children respond to teachers' statements, questions, and actions.

Organize a group of teachers to evaluate whether their program's management policies and practices meet children's needs. Ask them to suggest helpful changes or additions to planning documents, procedures for making and sharing portfolios, and assessment and reporting systems. Have group members prepare a written report about suggested program management changes and meet with the director to present their findings.

Plan a series of workshops on the managerial skills that teachers use. Discuss such skills as team building, observing and taking notes, analyzing information, managing time, using a planning cycle, and recordkeeping.

Completing Module 13: Professionalism

Module Sections	What Teachers Do	What Trainers Do
Overview **Viewing Yourself as a Professional** **Pre-Training Assessment**	Read about the standards, ethics, and obligations of the early childhood profession. Read and respond to questions about the three examples of how teachers maintain a commitment to professionalism; reflect on what it means to be a professional; and think about the interests, knowledge, skills, and style they bring to their work. Complete the *Pre-Training Assessment* and list 3–5 skills to improve or topics to learn more about. Share responses and chart feedback.	Observe teachers and review ongoing notes. Discuss with teachers • responses to questions about the examples • their understandings of themselves as professionals, including the skills and talents they bring to their work • the *Pre-Training Assessment* When possible, evaluate *Pre-Training Assessment* responses by observing.
Learning Activity A, Meeting Professional Standards	Read about the standards that guide the early childhood profession. Obtain and read a publication related to developmentally appropriate practice in programs for infants and toddlers. Describe how they apply the principles of good practice in their daily work. Share responses and chart feedback.	If necessary, help teachers obtain copies of the materials. Discuss the ideas teachers chose and how they are implementing them in their programs.
Learning Activity B, Continuing to Gain New Knowledge and Skills	Read about the four stages of professional development for teachers, the benefits of continued learning, joining professional groups, and other ways to continue professional growth. Select and learn about one early childhood professional organization. Develop a professional development plan that includes short- and long-term goals and ways of overcoming obstacles. Share responses and chart feedback.	Encourage teachers to build time for training and skill development into their schedules. Provide information about relevant classes, lectures, and conferences. Review teachers' professional development plans and offer support if necessary.

Completing Module 13: Professionalism (continued)

Module Sections	What Teachers Do	What Trainers Do
Learning Activity C, Behaving Ethically in Your Work	Read about the NAEYC *Code of Ethical Conduct*, examples of professional and unprofessional behavior, and situations that present ethical dilemmas. List examples of ways their behavior upholds the ethical principles of teaching. Share responses and chart feedback.	Discuss examples of professional behavior. Review observation notes to identify and share examples of teachers' commitment to ethical principles. Discuss ethical issues as they arise. Encourage teachers by acknowledging their conscientious work habits, ethical behavior, and continuing professional growth.
Learning Activity D, Talking About the Value of Your Work	Read about the importance of sharing their knowledge of early childhood care and education with others and about ways to advocate for change. Answer questions explaining the value of their work and their ideas about improving the early childhood field. Identify and take two advocacy steps and report the results of their efforts. Share responses and chart feedback.	Explain the importance of advocating in a way that is comfortable for them. Suggest ways to talk about the value of their work in the larger community. Review advocacy plans and offer to assist implementation.
Reflecting on Your Learning	Review responses to the *Pre-Training Assessment*, summarize progress by answering questions, and consider curriculum connections and partnerships with families. Share responses and chart feedback. Complete the knowledge assessment.	Discuss teachers' progress summaries. Give and score the *Knowledge Assessment* and provide feedback.

Strategies to Extend Learning

Facilitate a discussion about issues affecting the well-being of children and families in the community or state. Discuss ways for teachers to become advocates. Include a discussion of the importance of regarding infant and toddler teachers as early childhood professionals. Have teachers think about and explain whether people who work with infants and toddlers should be called *teachers*, *caregivers*, or another term.

Build a comprehensive lending library of professional materials. Include books, journals, and audiovisual materials about early childhood development and education, cultural competence, including children with disabilities, involving families, and other topics of interest to teachers.

Encourage teachers to be partners in each other's professional development. They might share rides and child care, plan and lead workshops together, share resources, and otherwise help each other achieve their professional goals.

Conduct workshops on ethical issues. Consider topics such as disciplinary methods or how to respond when teachers and parents disagree about appropriate practices. Ask teachers to suggest topics that they would like to discuss.

Discuss with teachers the next steps in their professional development. For example, will they seek a credential, attend college courses, enroll in a degree program, or continue independent study? Help teachers understand how these modules fit their plans for ongoing professional growth.

Chapter 3

Using the Modules in Courses and Workshops

When you use the *Caring for Infants & Toddlers* modules in group settings such as courses and workshops, consider the personal nature of the training program. In their *Skill-Building Journals*, teachers report their personal impressions and experiences, as well as how they apply information in their own settings. You will learn a great deal about each person and have a unique opportunity to adapt your training to address their individual interests and needs. Also keep in mind the value of observing teachers while they work with children. While group sessions can provide valuable information about each teacher's progress, the training is most effective when it includes individualized, on-site feedback and support based on systematic, objective observations. If you teach a college course, you may already observe teachers as part of a practicum. Use such visits to observe and to provide support and feedback, and use one to administer each *Competency Assessment*. The chart on page 11 shows how the 13 modules in *Caring for Infants & Toddlers* might be used for a series of college courses.

This chapter provides logistical tips to help you plan group sessions. It also offers suggestions to make people feel comfortable about participating. A variety of training approaches are described so you can use those that fit your style and what you know about the teachers who will be attending your sessions. We offer suggestions about evaluating the training and include a sample evaluation form in the Appendix. We also provide a sample training plan for module 6, *Communication*, to show how you might design a series of sessions on any of the 13 modules.

Attending to Logistics

Group sessions are most successful when they are well planned and everything is in place before participants arrive for training. What may seem like simple details can either enhance or interfere with learning. Here are some pointers for making logistical arrangements that support comfortable and productive training sessions.

- Schedule sessions at times that are convenient for teachers. For example, you might conduct them after the children leave for the day, at naptime, or, if possible, on in-service days. Teachers have steady demands on their professional and personal time. Accommodating their schedules is respectful, and it makes high attendance easier.

- Notify participants of the date, time, and location of the training. If appropriate, include directions to the building and room where the session will be held. Provide an agenda and other preparatory materials in advance.

- Offer refreshments. Healthy snacks and hot or cold drinks refresh minds and energize participants. A table cloth, even fresh flowers, can make the room inviting.

- Arrange for tables that seat 4–5 people and adult-size chairs that provide comfortable support.

- Prepare or arrange for needed materials and equipment in advance. This includes audiovisual equipment, videos, chart paper, markers, tape, chalk, handouts, and evaluation forms. Check to make sure the equipment works and that there are replacement bulbs, extension cords, and adapters on hand.

- Arrange the furniture before the participants arrive in a pattern that suits your training style. Many trainers prefer circles, semi-circles, or small tables because these arrangements encourage participant discussions.

- Display name tags, sign-in sheets, agendas, and reference materials in areas readily accessible to participants.

- Check to be sure the room temperature is comfortable before starting the session. An overheated room can put an audience to sleep more quickly than a boring speaker, but participants will have a hard time focusing if the room is too cold.

By attending to these few logistical concerns, you'll be able to focus on the content of the training rather than searching for extension cords or a building engineer to adjust the temperature. Preparation goes a long way when it comes to training.

Facilitating Group Sessions

One of your most important roles is to help all participants feel comfortable enough to express their ideas, share experiences, and ask questions. Some teachers find participation in group discussions and activities intimidating, and even experienced teachers may be reluctant to speak in a group. Here are some tips for facilitating training sessions that will help participants feel comfortable about participating.

At the Start of the Session

- Greet participants by name as they enter. Welcome them to the session.

- Discuss the rules and guidelines, describe the plan for breaks, and say when the session will end.

- Point out the location of restrooms, telephones, and water fountains. This will minimize interruptions once the session starts.

- Provide an overview of the session. Explain the goals and objectives, describe the content and activities, and refer to the handouts. Invite participants to share their own expectations. Training is more effective when the group understands and shares a commitment to the goals and objectives.

- Remind participants that they are responsible for their own learning. Explain that everyone will take something different from the session, depending on what ideas are most important to them, how much they contribute, and whether they integrate and use what they learn.

- Underscore the importance of the topics and skills to be covered. Emphasize that the purpose of training is to help teachers do their jobs better and enhance their professional development.

During Discussions

- Encourage participants to listen actively and to express their opinions. Acknowledge that sharing ideas and experiences in a group may feel a little uncomfortable at first. Note that all ideas are valuable and there is usually more than one right way to approach a topic. Avoid embarrassing participants by forcing each person to contribute.

- Look for body-language cues. They may alert you to discomfort with the subject matter (squirming), shyness about contributing (avoiding eye contact), or anger (turning the entire body away). Try to respond to what you see.

- Guide participants to reach compromises or at least to respect different points of view. This is particularly important when conflicts or disagreements occur.

- Encourage participants to ask questions. Answering their questions helps you explain information and eliminate misunderstandings. It is often helpful to rephrase questions to clarify what is being asked. Redirect some questions to the group to help participants find answers on the basis of their own experiences and expertise. If you can't answer a question, say so and explain that you will try to find the answer before the next session. Be sure to follow up.

- Ask questions to engage teachers in dialogue. At times, it is appropriate to use both closed questions ("What happened when you handled the situation that way last time?") and open-ended questions ("What are some other ways you could handle the situation?"). Refer a question to the entire group if you sense that an in-depth discussion would be beneficial. ("That's a tough problem. Does anyone have a suggestion?")

Throughout the Session

- Draw on participants' experiences. Training is more meaningful when participants relate concepts to personal situations and experiences.

- Emphasize skill development rather than rote learning of correct responses. Learning is the process of assimilating new information and using it to improve skills.

- Encourage participants to make interpretations and draw conclusions. Effective training provides background information; data; and examples participants use to identify patterns or trends, make generalizations, and draw conclusions.

- Adjust the agenda to meet the needs of participants. Use a mixture of planned and spontaneous activities and content, just as you take advantage of teachable moments with children.

- Use small-group activities to discuss feelings. Consider using role-playing, simulations, or problem-solving assignments.

- Give clear instructions for activities. Repeat them if necessary. Move around the room to assist individuals or groups who are confused about the tasks.

- Review and summarize each section of the training before moving on to the next. At the end of the session, lead a summary discussion and answer participants' questions.

- Be available during breaks to discuss issues and topics. Some participants may prefer to share their views with you one-on-one rather than in front of the whole group.

Varying Training Approaches

There are many training techniques to consider as you plan group training based on the *Caring for Infants & Toddlers* modules. Select training techniques that reflect current knowledge about how adults learn, address the needs of the teachers who will participate, and are consistent with your own preferences and training philosophy. For example, you may want to plan mini-lectures as part of your workshops if you are comfortable giving presentations. On the other hand, you may rely on group discussions if are unsure of your skills as a lecturer. Your range of training approaches should meet participants' varied learning styles.

Include a variety of activities and use different kinds of media when possible. A balance of training techniques maintains the group's interest and promotes greater retention and application of skills and content. To encourage participants' active involvement, consider using role-playing, small group analysis, discussion, and case studies. These techniques allow participants to apply training concepts, principles, and strategies to real-life situations.

Try those of the following training ideas that suit your style and what you know about the participants. Make modifications as necessary.

Written Materials

When using the modules for training, make sure that every participant has a copy of the *Skill-Building Journal*. Participants will also need to have access to *Caring for Infants & Toddlers* so they can do the readings. You can supplement these resources with articles from professional journals, a list of Web sites, or some of the resources recommended at the back of the book.

Audiovisuals

Audiovisuals can be very effective training tools. Videotapes that show realistic and relevant scenes from early childhood programs are especially effective. Your own slides or videotapes of programs can be used to illustrate ideas covered in training.

Some trainers use visual displays, such as PowerPoint presentations or overhead transparencies, to reinforce the key points of a lecture and introduce discussion topics and questions. Either format can include both words and pictures, but PowerPoint presentations offer more creative and sophisticated options. Here are some suggestions for developing slides and transparencies.

- Include key words and phrases only.

- Use large type so participants can read the screen from anywhere in the room.

- Be sure there is sufficient contrast between the background color and lettering so text is easy to read.

- Keep illustrations or graphs simple.

- Use color to highlight key information.

- Use visuals, such as photographs, to introduce and reinforce content.

Problem-Solving Activities

One popular and effective training technique is group problem solving. Brainstorming solutions to realistic problems can energize a group and generate many ideas. Brainstorming is designed to separate the creation of ideas from their evaluation. This strategy works best in groups of 5–12 persons and requires someone to serve as the recorder and someone to be the facilitator who leads the group through the process. The rules for brainstorming are as follows:

- All ideas are listed; no critical remarks are allowed.

- *Hitchhiking* is allowed; if one participant can improve upon or combine previously mentioned ideas, so much the better.

- *Freewheeling* is encouraged; even outlandish ideas keep the group momentum going.

- There is no limit to the number of ideas that may be included. The more ideas that participants generate, the more likely viable solutions will evolve.

- Discussion and evaluation are postponed until participants have finished generating ideas.

Brainstorming could be used to answer questions such as the following:

- Why do children misbehave?

- What factors work against families' participation in the program?

- What are the best ways to keep children engaged in listening to a story?

Case Studies

Case studies are realistic examples of situations related to a particular topic. The chief advantage of this method is that it helps participants apply what they learn through lectures or assigned readings to the real world. Many of the vignettes and examples in the modules can be used to develop case studies.

Distribute a copy of the case study to each participant or small group and allow time for it to be read. Participants can discuss the study in pairs, small groups, or the full group. Depending on the case study, ask leading questions to stimulate thinking. Here are some examples:

- What went wrong?

- What worked well?

- How could this problem be avoided in the future?

- How could this individual build on his or her success?

- What did the children learn from this experience?

- What feedback would you provide to this individual?

Role-Playing

Role-playing presents opportunities to act out real-life situations in a risk-free environment. By seeing things from another perspective, participants gain insight into various ways to approach a problem or issue. Keep in mind that some adults are very uncomfortable playing different roles and may prefer to watch. A more comfortable way to conduct role-playing is to form groups of three, with two persons assuming roles and the third person observing and giving feedback.

Discussion Techniques

Trainers can use fishbowl, fantasy, and visualization techniques to stimulate discussions. For the **fishbowl**, divide participants into two groups, forming inner and outer rings of a circle. Give participants in the inner group an assignment based on the content of the training. For example, the inner group might discuss the difference between discipline and punishment. While the inner group discusses this problem for five to ten minutes, the outer group observes. At the end of the allotted time, the two groups switch roles. At the conclusion of the second discussion, both groups comment on what they observed. This technique can stimulate discussion among participants who are reluctant to speak in a large group.

Fantasy and visualization are techniques used to draw on right brain (creative thinking) powers. **Fantasy** techniques usually ask participants to reflect on "What if . . .?" situations, for example, "What if you had unlimited financial resources? How would you equip your room?" Participants can list the materials and equipment in an ideal inventory and then compare the ideal to reality to see where compromises are appropriate. Conversely, you can fantasize about worst-case scenarios: "What if your budget were cut by 50 percent?"

Visualization allows participants to use their imaginations to think about a task and relate it to past or future experiences. For example, you might ask participants to think about a time when they had to do something that made them uncomfortable. What were the circumstances? How did they feel? What did they do to relieve their discomfort? What will they do if it ever happens again? You might use visualization if you sense that participants are uncomfortable dealing with particular situations, such as explaining to parents that children may not attend the program when they have a contagious illness.

Mini-Lectures

Mini-lectures are useful when you are covering important points that you want everyone to understand. Provide a handout summarizing the key ideas or refer participants to where the ideas are discussed in *Caring for Infants & Toddlers*. Illustrate key concepts with visuals such as PowerPoint presentations, overhead transparencies, or notes recorded on chart paper.

At the close of the mini-lecture, review the key points. You can restate them yourself, invite the group to summarize, conduct a review discussion, or lead an activity related to the material. These steps allow participants to assimilate the ideas and construct their own understandings. They can relate it to their own thinking, decide what it means to them, and consider how it affects their work with children and families.

Group Discussions

Small groups of 4–6 participants are ideal for discussion and sharing. For participants who are reluctant to speak in a large group, small-group activities are more comfortable. Small-group interactions offer more intimate connections among group members, encourage the active involvement of all participants, and help them build networks and relationships.

To form small groups, try one of the following methods:

- Ask participants to form groups of a specified size.

- Have participants count off (e.g., up to 5) and then group persons with the same number.

- Distribute cards with pictures, stickers, or numbers and have participants match cards and group accordingly.

- Assign participants to groups according to roles or ability.

- Distribute individual pieces of 4- to 6-piece puzzles. Participants form groups by assembling the puzzles.

- Place pictures or names of classifiable objects in a bag (for example, furniture, clothing, animals). Have participants choose a card and then form a group with others whose objects fit the same category.

Here are some strategies for using small groups effectively:

- Give clear instructions for the task and check to be sure participants understand what they are to do.

- Seat participants together and away from other groups.

- Give 3- and 1-minute warnings before ending discussions.

- Ask groups to report to the whole group in round-robin style. Each group takes a turn reporting one or two ideas until all new ideas are listed. This prevents repetition, and the first group does not report all the popular answers.

- Reporting to the full group may not always be necessary, especially if you think that each group's discussion was thorough. Ask if there were any highlights or important insights any group would like to share.

Large-group discussions can be used to break up a mini-lecture, discuss reactions to a videotape, and give participants an opportunity to contribute to and learn from their peers. If an entire group is 15 persons or less, discussions involving the whole group allow members to hear all the ideas.

The trainer's role is to facilitate communication and make sure everyone can hear. It is important to receive participants' comments without judgment. If a statement indicates a lack of understanding, use the next break to discuss it with the participant. If a statement is incorrect, provide the correct information as diplomatically as possible: "Many people think that is true; however, the state health office recommends..."

During large-group discussions, some participants might be frustrated because they feel ignored, misunderstood, or unable to participate. It is important to observe both the behavior of the group as a whole and that of individuals. When a participant's comments have apparently been misunderstood, paraphrase and clarify them for the whole group: "What I hear you saying is... Am I right?" This strategy allows participants to restate their comments and continue to participate.

Evaluating Training

Trainers want to know if their training has been effective. Did the participants increase their understanding of the content? Do they feel capable of implementing what they have learned? Do they think the session was beneficial? Did they gain skills or change approaches?

To answer these questions, you can use group or individual training evaluations. The following are two examples of evaluation techniques that involve the whole group in offering feedback during a training session.

Pluses and Wishes: On chart paper or a blackboard, draw a chart with two columns. Label one "pluses" and the other "wishes." Ask, "What did you like about this training? What were the pluses? What do you wish the training had included but did not?" Responses are likely to vary from concerns about logistics ("The chairs were uncomfortable.") to comments about the content ("I can use the ideas for making prop boxes immediately.").

Gets/Wants Chart: On chart paper or a blackboard, make a chart with four quadrants, like the axes on a graph. Label the sections as in the following example.

Got—Wanted	**Didn't Get—Wanted**
Suggestions for encouraging creativity *Opportunities to learn from other teachers*	*Ideas for new materials* *Refreshments*

Got—Didn't Want	**Didn't Get—Didn't Want**
Video I'd seen before *Role-playing*	

As you discuss each quadrant, ask participants to provide examples of parts of the training they "got and wanted," "got but didn't want," and "didn't get but wanted." When you get to the last quadrant, explain that it doesn't need to be addressed because the items must be irrelevant to their jobs ("You didn't get this information, but it doesn't matter because you didn't want it!"). See the chart above for examples of the types of responses participants might offer. When planning future training, you can review the responses and decide if you should continue to offer the things they "got and wanted," provide things they "didn't get and wanted," and eliminate the things they "got and didn't want!"

Individual questionnaires completed at the end of the training can help you assess which parts of the training were well received. (A sample training evaluation questionnaire is provided in the Appendix.) For example, did participants like group exercises but dislike the mini-lectures? Did they think too much content was presented in too short a time? Review participants' reactions to answer questions such as these:

- How effectively did the session accomplish its objectives?

- How relevant was the content to the participants' jobs?

- What changes to the format, content, activities, or techniques are needed?

- Do participants need more in-depth coverage of the topic?

Participant evaluations are a valuable tool for assessing whether training needs have been met. As you review the results, though, bear in mind that not everyone is always going to be satisfied with training. Some variations in answers are to be expected, and you should revise your approach only if warranted.

Sample Training Plan for Module 6, *Communication*

When planning a series of group sessions based on the modules in *Caring for Infants & Toddlers*, think about the training techniques you will use, how you will facilitate discussions, and how you will evaluate the sessions. Before each session, ask participants to submit their completed *Skill-Building Journal* forms for your review and written comments. Explain that you will return their work, with your comments, at the beginning of the session. Be sure to allow time for participants to take a quick look at your comments before the session begins. Develop a plan to meet individually with teachers who would like assistance in completing an activity or who want to discuss your feedback.

An example of a plan for a series of group sessions on module 6, *Communication*, follows. This plan can be adapted to address individual interests and training needs. A "Planning Form for Group Sessions" is in the Appendix. You may find this form helpful as a framework for planning group sessions on any of the *Caring for Infants & Toddlers* modules.

Sample Training Plan for Module 6, *Communication*

Overview

Open the Session

Begin with an open-ended question such as the following:

- What is communication?

- What are some verbal and nonverbal ways that people communicate?

- How do babies communicate what they feel, want, and need?

- How do you support children's language development?

Discuss the Key Topics

Introduce the three major areas in which teachers develop competence to promote communication skills and guide children's language development. These areas are

- creating places where infants and toddlers can enjoy sounds, language, pictures, and print

- offering opportunities for infants and toddlers to explore sounds, language, pictures, and print

- encouraging and responding to infants' and toddlers' efforts to communicate

Lead a discussion about the key topics by using questions such as the following:

- How do infants and toddlers learn about sounds, language, pictures, and print?

  Possible responses:

  They notice sounds in their indoor and outdoor environments, including language, music, and natural sounds.

  They have verbal and non-verbal, back and forth exchanges with their families and teachers.

  They look at photographs of themselves, their families, and familiar objects.

  They point to familiar objects in books and ask, "What's that?"

  They begin to experiment with drawing, painting, and writing tools.

- How do you encourage and respond to infants' and toddlers' efforts to communicate?

  Possible responses:

  When babies cry, I figure out what their cries mean. If they want to be changed or fed, held, or put down, I respond as quickly as possible. I also tell them what I think they are trying to communicate. I might say, "Oh, you're hungry, so you want your bottle."

  I show children that their home language is important to me by learning some key words in their language.

  I describe what we are doing. For example, I might say, "Oops. Your pants got muddy on the playground. Mommy sent some clean pants. Let's put them on. First let's get the muddy ones off. Here comes one leg. Now let's get the other leg in there."

  I make up silly rhymes with children's names.

  I have lots of books in the room, and I like to sit with a child on the glider, reading that child's favorite story again and again.

Discuss the Three Stories

Discuss the story about how Ms. Gonzalez encouraged Lovette to use language and to explore books.

- Ask participants to offer examples of how they encourage the children in their group to use language and to explore books.

- Discuss the example and responses to the questions in the *Skill-Building Journal*.

- Invite participants to describe a similar situation in their program, how they handled it, and what happened.

Discuss the story about how Ms. Gonzalez and Mr. Lewis encouraged Jessica and Adam to use language and explore writing.

- Ask participants to give examples of the ways they encourage children to use language and explore writing.

- Discuss the example and responses to the questions in the *Skill-Building Journal*.

- Invite participants to describe a similar situation in their program, how they handled it, and what happened.

Discuss the story about Mr. Lewis's conversation with Sammy.

- Ask participants how they let children know that they are listening to them.

- Discuss the example and responses to the questions in the *Skill-Building Journal*.

- Invite participants to describe a similar situation in their program, how they handled it, and what happened.

Discuss Your Own Experiences With Communication

Lead a discussion about the four aspects of verbal communication: listening, talking, reading, and writing. Use questions such as the following to encourage participation:

- How do you send clear messages?

  Possible responses:

    I try to say what I mean directly, so I won't be misinterpreted.

    If I need help, I ask for it directly.

    Sometimes I ask questions about what I said, to check whether the other person understood my meaning.

    I sometimes write things down to make sure that I am saying them clearly and to make sure that I remember everything I want to say.

- How do you use reading to learn about the world, do your job better, and explore your interests?

  Possible responses:

    I subscribe to a news magazine.

    I find articles on the Internet about working with infants and toddlers. I try to read one article a week.

    I read cookbooks and cooking magazines to find new recipes to try at home.

    I love to read mysteries.

Invite participants to share their answers to the *Skill-Building Journal* questions about their own experiences with communication.

End the Session

Answer questions. Schedule individual meetings or phone conferences to discuss responses and concerns. Review the teachers' *Pre-Training Assessments* and their lists of skills to improve or topics to learn more about. Direct teachers to *Learning Activity A.*

Learning Activity A

Using Your Knowledge of Infants and Toddlers to Promote Communication Skills

Open the Session

Ask participants how their knowledge of infants and toddlers helps them promote communication skills.

Possible responses:

I have a practical understanding of what children can do, so I don't expect too much or too little.

I understand that infants and toddlers can communicate a great deal, even when they can't talk yet.

I know that infants may explore books and crayons by smelling and tasting them, before they turn the pages or make marks with the crayon.

I provide different kinds of books for young infants, mobile infants, and toddlers. I give very young infants washable cloth and plastic books to explore. When their fine motor skills grow, I give them board books so they can turn the pages. I give older infants books with simple pictures of familiar objects. For toddlers, I add picture books with simple plots.

I observe children to see if there are any developmental alerts that I should talk to families about. If necessary, I suggest that they talk to their health care provider.

Emphasize the importance of supporting children's communication skills. Tell participants about the study by Betty Hart and Todd R. Risley, who found that children whose parents spent the most time talking to them had much larger vocabularies and did better in school than children who had fewer verbal interactions.[1]

Ask participants to think about and share the implications of this study for teachers.

Possible responses:

It's very important for teachers to listen to and talk with children. We can talk about almost anything and everything.

We can play with language and use interesting words to help children develop their vocabularies. For example, during meals and snacks, we can name the foods children are eating and describe them as delicious, yummy, tasty, crunchy, and so on.

If we work with children whose families have fewer verbal interactions with them, we deliberately have to help children catch up with their more verbal peers.

We can also support children's language development by singing, saying rhymes, and reading aloud with them.

Discuss the Text

Review the contents of the section "Development: It's All Connected" on page 191 of *Caring for Infants & Toddlers*. Ask participants for additional examples of how the development of communication skills is related to physical, cognitive, self, and social development.

Call participants' attention to the chart "Some Language and Communication Development Alerts" on page 192 of *Caring for Infants & Toddlers*. Remind them that it is important to be careful observers of children and that it is important to know when to suggest that a family talk to their health care provider about a possible language and communication delay.

Review the Activity

Review and discuss the content of the charts, "Using Your Knowledge of Young Infants," "Using Your Knowledge of Mobile Infants," and "Using Your Knowledge of Toddlers." Ask participants to share examples of what they do to support children's language development.

Offer Additional Resources and Activities

Provide chart paper or poster board and markers so participants can make charts similar to those in this learning activity. Suggest posting them in a central area, such as the staff lounge, so they and their colleagues can add additional examples of what infants and toddlers are like and ways to use this information to promote communication skills.

End the Session

Offer to review and discuss the completed activity during individual meetings or phone conferences.

Give a brief overview of the next learning activity.

Learning Activity B

Creating an Environment That Invites Infants and Toddlers to Enjoy Sounds, Language, Pictures, and Print

Open the Session

Begin by asking participants to work in groups to brainstorm a list of the sounds, language, pictures, and print they paid attention to that day.

Possible responses:

On my early morning walk, I heard birds singing, dogs barking, and cars honking.

I read the cereal box at breakfast and the lunch menu at a fast food restaurant.

I talked to my mother on the telephone this morning and talked to my children while they were getting ready for school.

I listened to music on my car radio while I was driving to work.

Review the following key points:

- The environment can encourage communication and invite infants and toddlers to explore language.

- Teachers are the most important part of the language-learning environment for infants and toddlers.

- There are many strategies for setting up the environment to encourage listening, talking, reading, and writing.

Discuss the Text

To encourage participants to share their ideas, ask questions such as the following:

- What strategies do you use to encourage children to listen and talk?

Possible responses:

I have a gliding rocker in the room so a child can sit in my lap to listen to a story.

In my toddler room, I have an area for imitating and pretending. I have a great collection of hats, tote bags, and dress-up clothes for the toddlers to use. They love to talk on the toy telephones.

I have a picture of every child's family in the room. Some are at floor level, where children who crawl can see them. Others are higher up, where they can be seen by a baby I am carrying.

I sing lullabies to children when I put them in their cribs to sleep.

- How do you use the environment to support children's exploration of reading and writing?

  Possible responses:

  I made a book for each child, with pictures of the child and the other people in the family. I even included pictures of their pets.

  I have picture and word labels on my shelves so children know where to put things back.

  I have a cozy book area. I've covered a lot of the books with clear adhesive paper so I don't have to worry about children's tearing the covers.

  When we go outdoors, I give the children large paint brushes and water so they can paint the fence. I also have large chunks of chalk for them to use.

  I have lots of materials that help children develop small muscle skills, such as puzzles, beads, small blocks, large pegs, and nesting cups. Small muscle skills allow children to manipulate print materials and writing, drawing, and painting tools.

Review the Activity

Ask participants to work in pairs or groups of three to share their responses to the *Skill-Building Journal* charts "Encouraging Language Skills" and "Encouraging Emerging Literacy Learning." Suggest that participants add their partners' ideas to the column "What Else We Could Do." Have participants write down the two or three new ideas that they would like to implement first. Offer support as necessary to help teachers carry out their ideas.

Offer Additional Resources and Activities

Offer to help teachers evaluate how well their environments support language development by providing an instrument such as the *Infant/Toddler Environment Rating Scale.*[2] Share books that stress the importance of language development, such as *Meaningful Differences in the Lives of Young American Children.*[3] Discuss ways to involve families as partners in helping children develop communication skills.

End the Session

Offer to review and discuss the completed activity during individual meetings or phone conferences.

Give a brief overview of the next learning activity.

Learning Activity C

Encouraging the Language Development of Infants and Toddlers

Open the Session

Begin by asking participants to think about the language development of a child they know well. Ask questions such as the following to encourage participants to share their experiences:

- What were the first vocal sounds you remember hearing the child make?

- How did you know what the child was communicating before he or she used words?

- What was the child's first word? Why do you think he or she said that word first?

- Did you speak parentese to the child? Why or why not?

- Did you play games such as "This Little Piggy Went to Market" or "Pat-a-Cake" with the child? If so, what was the child's reaction?

Discuss the Text

Divide participants into groups of three. Assign one person in each group to reread, take notes, and become the group's expert on one of the following sections in the text:

- The first person rereads the suggestions to support language development on pages 199–200 of the text.

- The second person rereads the section "Serving as a Language Model," which is on pages 200–201 of the text.

- The third person's assignment is the section "Engaging Children as Conversational Partners," which is on page 201 of the text.

Once participants have finished rereading their sections, ask each person to review the important points in the selection they read with the others on their team. Encourage the participants to ask questions and discuss the ideas presented in the book. Ask them to share additional ways to model language, engage children in conversation, and otherwise support language development.

Conduct a brief discussion about children who are learning one language at home and a different language at the program. Invite participants to share their experiences with children who are learning more than one language. Emphasize the following key points:

- Although families (and teachers) may be concerned that using children's home language might interfere with learning English, children's understanding of their home language actually helps them make sense of a second language.

- Children who are learning two languages may start talking a little later than those who are only learning one language. When they begin to talk, they are likely to use words from both languages.

- If you do not speak the child's home language, you can support children by learning some important words, phrases, and children's songs and rhymes in the home language.

- The ability to communicate in more than one language is a great benefit, and it is becoming more and more important in our global community.

Review the Activity

Ask participants to work in pairs for this activity. One person in each pair will be the reporter, and the other will be the listener. Instruct the reporter to read to her partner the notes on how she encouraged an infant's or toddler's language development for three days. Ask the partner to listen and, while listening, to think about the experience through the eyes of the child. Then ask the listener to describe to her partner what she thinks the child might have been feeling, thinking, and learning. Ask partners to compare the listener's answer to the reporter's response to the relevant question in the *Skill-Building Journal*. Then instruct partners to change roles and repeat the process.

Additional Resources and Activities

If participants are working with children who are learning one language at home and another in the program, invite a parent or other person who speaks the home language to teach words, phrases, songs, and rhymes to both the teachers and the children. Guide an Internet search for sources of simple children's books in the home languages. Invite parents to record words, stories, songs, and rhymes to play for the children during the day.

End the Session

Offer to review and discuss the completed activity during individual meetings or phone conferences.

Give a brief overview of the next learning activity.

Learning Activity D

Sharing Books With Infants and Toddlers

Open the Session

Ask participants to talk about their favorite children's books and explain why they like those particular books. (Allow participants to pass if they cannot think of a book just then.)

Review the following key points:

- It is never too soon to begin reading aloud to children. Even the youngest children enjoy listening to voices and language.

- The more children are read to, the more likely they are to become good readers.

- Reading aloud is one of the best ways to ensure children's later success as readers.

Discuss the Text

Remind participants that *Learning Activity D* discusses how to select and provide books that are appropriate for infants and toddlers, and how to read aloud to very young children.

To encourage participants to think about appropriate books, divide them into small groups and give each group a collection of children's books. Ask participants to evaluate the books, using the charts on pages 205 and 206 of *Caring for Infants & Toddlers*. Ask each group to decide whether the books are appropriate for infants, for toddlers, for both infants and toddlers, or not at all appropriate for this age group. Invite each group to share one appropriate and one inappropriate book. Encourage them to explain their reasoning.

Ask questions such as the following to encourage participants to share their ideas about reading aloud with infants and toddlers:

- Why should you read aloud to infants and toddlers?

    Possible responses:

    They learn listening skills.

    They learn new words.

    They begin to understand how books and print work.

    They will learn to think that reading is fun.

Conduct an activity such as the following to emphasize the importance of reading aloud to infants and toddlers:

- Before the session, prepare four sheets of chart paper. Write one of the following headings on each sheet, using a different colored marker for each heading: "Reading to Mobile Infants," "Before You Read to Toddlers," "While Reading to Toddlers," and "After Reading to Toddlers." Post these sheets on the wall of the training room.

- Divide participants into four groups and give each group one of the markers. Give the following directions:

    Find the chart with the heading written in the same colored marker as the one your group was given.

    Move to the chart and choose a recorder for your group.

    You will have two minutes at each chart to think about and record strategies you use for reading to infants and toddlers.

- Call time after each 2-minute interval. Ask the groups to take their markers and move to the next chart. Allow time for participants to read the existing list and add new ideas. Continue in a similar manner until all groups have visited each chart once. Allow additional time for all participants to walk around the room, reviewing the charts.

Review the Activity

Ask participants to work in pairs or small groups to share and discuss their experiences reading with an individual child and with a small group of toddlers. Ask if there are any volunteers to who would like to read aloud to the group. Encourage them to explain what they would do before and after they read aloud.

Offer Additional Resources and Activities

If you have access to a video camera, offer to videotape participants as they read a story with an infant or a group of toddlers. Invite them to watch the videotape with a colleague and to think about changes they would like to make in how they get ready to read, while reading, or after reading to children.

End the Session

Offer to review and discuss the completed activity during individual meetings or phone conferences.

Give a brief overview of the section *Reflecting on Your Learning*.

Concluding the Module

Reflecting on Your Learning

Return participants' completed activity forms and progress summaries with your comments. Offer to review and discuss them during individual meetings or phone conferences.

Ask participants to share something they learned while working on this module.

Ask participants to share some of the ways they adapted or changed their approach to promoting infants' and toddlers' communication skills. How have they changed their environment to invite children to enjoy sounds, language, pictures, and print? Have they changed their practices in reading aloud? If so, how?

Ask volunteers to share a few examples of the curriculum connections they explored.

Ask volunteers to share a few examples of how they shared something they learned with families.

Ask volunteers to share something they want to learn more about and how they propose to learn about it.

End the Session

Return participants' completed activity forms and progress summaries with your comments. Offer to review and discuss these during individual meetings or phone conferences.

Schedule individual meetings with teachers to review their progress. Also schedule and conduct the knowledge and competency assessments, and offer feedback as the assessments are undertaken. Remind participants to update their "Individual Tracking Forms."

---

[1] Hart, B., & Risley, T. R. (1995). *Meaningful differences in the everyday experiences of young American children.* Baltimore: Paul H. Brookes Publishing Co.

[2] Harms, T., Cryer, D., & Clifford, R. M. (2003). *Infant/toddler environment rating scale* (Rev. ed.). New York, NY: Teachers College Press.

[3] Op cit.

Chapter 4

Chapter 4 (continued)

Assessing Each Teacher's Progress

The *Caring for Infants & Toddlers* training program includes two types of assessment for each module. *Knowledge Assessments* test a teacher's understanding of the information presented in the module. *Competency Assessments* require a teacher to apply knowledge and skills while working with children and families. For each module, the criteria for the competency assessment are drawn from the *Pre-Training Assessment*, and they are observable. Modules 1–12 include both knowledge and competency assessments. Module 13 has only a knowledge assessment because mastery of the skills developed through the module cannot be readily determined during an observation period.

This chapter describes the role of the trainer in the assessment process. It includes the *Knowledge Assessment* for each module, *Knowledge Assessment Answer Sheets* to facilitate scoring, and the *Competency Assessment* observation forms.

The Assessment Process

Trainers administer the assessments after teachers have successfully completed all sections of a module: the *Overview*, the section on personal experiences, the *Pre-Training Assessment*, the learning activities, and *Reflecting on Your Learning*. During individual meetings, you meet with teachers to discuss their responses to the progress summary questions and review the strategies listed in the *Pre-Training Assessment* for the module. You discuss and jointly decide whether the teacher is ready for the assessments. (Having provided feedback on all the learning activities, you will already have a good idea whether an individual is ready.) If a teacher is not ready for assessment, you can suggest repeating one or more learning activities or provide additional training resources. If the decision is to proceed with the assessments, schedule times to administer them.

The assessment process is designed as another learning experience. If a teacher seems anxious, explain that continued support is available if his or her performance on either assessment is not successful. Reassure the individual that there will be additional opportunities to gain and demonstrate the necessary knowledge and skills.

Trainers will need to maintain a supply of the assessment forms, so it might be helpful to set up a filing system for storing copies of the *Knowledge Assessments* and *Competency Assessment* observation forms.

Administering the Knowledge Assessments

The *Knowledge Assessments* are paper-and-pencil exercises that test knowledge of the information and concepts presented in the module. They are open-book tests because the intention is to validate what the teacher understands. The questions, which are based on the *Overview* and learning activities, include multiple-choice, matching, short-answer, and extended-answer formats. Most teachers will need approximately 20–30 minutes of uninterrupted time to complete each *Knowledge Assessment*. You may administer it before or after the *Competency Assessment* observation.

It may have been a long a time since some teachers have taken a test. Reassure them that the purpose is to validate how much they have learned about a topic. Remind them to read each question completely before attempting to answer it. Also suggest that they review all of their answers before turning in the assessment. This will help them catch mistakes such as writing on the wrong line or misreading a question.

Conducting the Competency Assessments

The *Competency Assessment* observation forms are included at the end of this chapter. The form for each module includes a list of assessment criteria with spaces to indicate whether each criterion has been met, partially met, or not met. The *Competency Assessment* is scored on the basis of a scheduled, objective, systematic observation of a teacher while he or she works with children, as well as information you collected while working with the teacher on the module sections. The recommended observation period is one hour, but this will vary depending on the time of day, what the children are doing, and how often you have observed the teacher throughout the training program. You may want to observe at a particular time of day so you can witness a specific routine or activity (for example, you might want to observe arrival or departure times or outdoor play). For several modules, part of the competency assessment observation must be conducted at a specific time:

- Module 1, *Safe*, requires observation of an emergency drill.

- Module 11, *Families*, involves observation of drop-off or pick-up times.

- Module 12, *Program Management*, includes observation of a group of teachers planning together.

Read the criteria before the competency assessment observation and score any items that you can rate on the basis of your work with the teacher and previous observations of the teacher and the program environment. During the assessment observation, focus on the teacher's interactions with children, families, and other teachers. Take notes to document exactly what you see and hear so you can capture the teacher's interactions with and responses to children. Observation notes should provide objective descriptions of what you observed so you can share specific information with the teacher.

Useful observation notes are

- **Accurate:** Provide a factual and exact description of the teacher's and children's actions and language. Record what they do and say in the order in which they happen. Be specific. Try to include direct quotes whenever possible.

- **Objective:** Include only facts. Do not use labels, judgments, or inferences.

- **Complete:** Present a detailed picture of the setting, the number and ages of children, the teacher's actions and words, and the children's verbal and nonverbal responses. Describe the area in which the action took place and the materials and equipment in use. Include descriptions of activities from beginning to end.

Some of the competencies cannot be observed during the scheduled period. For these items, ask the teacher to show you any documents (e.g., portfolios of children's work, weekly planning forms, family communications) that demonstrate competence. You may also need to ask the teacher specific questions about particular items, such as established policies and procedures.

Scoring the Assessments

Most adults are eager to know the results of their work. Score the assessments and share the results with the teacher as soon as possible.

The *Answer Sheets* indicate how to score each *Knowledge Assessment* question. When a question has more than one possible correct response, this is noted on the *Answer Sheets*. A perfect score is 100. A teacher must obtain a score of at least 80 percent.

Here is a sample of a completed *Competency Assessment* observation form for module 10, *Guidance*.

---

10 Guidance

Competency Assessment

Teacher: Ms. Bates

Observer: Ms. Sanchez

Date/Time: 5-4-05 / 10:00-11:30 AM

Setting: Central Child Care, Room 3

Review your records from this observation and other information you collected while this teacher was working on module 10. Score each criterion of competence that you can substantiate.

Providing an Environment That Supports the Development of Self-Control

The competent teacher will:

check the appropriate box — met / partially met / not met

1. Provide safe, well-organized spaces that let children make choices and use materials. ☑ ☐ ☐
2. Follow a flexible schedule so teachers can respond promptly to children's needs. ☑ ☐ ☐
3. Plan daily routines and activities to minimize waiting time. ☐ ☑ ☐

To score the *Competency Assessment*, review your notes from the assessment observation, previous observations, your examination of the environment, the teacher's documents, and, if applicable, your interview with the teacher. Use your notes to decide whether each criterion of competence was met, partially met, or not met. If you did not observe a criterion, leave the rating blank. A teacher should successfully meet most (80 percent) of the criteria.

Sharing the Results

Schedule a meeting with the teacher to discuss the answers to the *Knowledge Assessment* and what you saw and heard during the *Competency Assessment* observation. Keep in mind that the purpose of the assessment process is to evaluate a teacher's understanding and application of the knowledge and skills presented in the module. In most cases, teachers already know whether they have mastered the needed knowledge and skills.

If the teacher has achieved a score of at least 80 percent on the *Knowledge Assessment*, offer your congratulations and briefly review any incorrect responses. If the teacher has not achieved a passing score, take your time going over the questions and answers so you can assess how much support the teacher needs to understand fully the material presented in the module. As stated earlier, the goal is to ensure competence and understanding, not simply to have the teacher pass the test. You might have the teacher repeat specific learning activities or read additional training resources.

Here is a possible approach to discussing the *Competency Assessment* results.

- **Begin by asking the teacher to comment on the observation period.** "Was today a typical day?" "Did everything go as you had planned?" "Were there any surprises?"

- **Discuss what went well and what problems existed, if any.** "What do you think went especially well?" "Is there anything you would want to do differently?"

- **Share your observation notes with the teacher.** "Let's look at my notes about what happened and see what we learn from them."

- **Review the criteria together.** Ask the teacher to assess which skills were clearly demonstrated and which were not.

- **Discuss your decision about the teacher's competence and explain the reasoning behind it.**

  If the teacher has clearly demonstrated competence, appears to understand the information, and applies it consistently while working with children, offer congratulations and take a few minutes to share observations of his or her progress.

  If the teacher has not met the criteria for competence, state your decision and explain why you think he or she needs more time to develop the necessary skills. Give examples from your observation notes. Ask what support would be most helpful and develop a plan to work together. Assure the teacher that the *Competency Assessment* may be rescored when his or her skills are stronger.

As teachers work on other modules, consider periodically reviewing their use of strategies from earlier modules. Your observations may sometimes indicate that a teacher needs to refresh knowledge and skills by reviewing learning activities already completed.

The following sections include copies of the *Knowledge Assessments*, *Answer Sheets* for all 13 modules, and the *Competency Assessment* observation forms for modules 1–12.

Knowledge Assessment   Module 1: Safe

You may use Caring for Infants & Toddlers *and your* Skill-Building Journal *to complete this assessment.*

Matching (5 points each)
Choose the lettered item in the right column that best matches each statement in the left column. Write the letter of your choice on the line next to the number of the statement.

___ 1. Infants investigate the world as soon as they can. They reach for and touch things they see, and they taste almost everything they hold.	(a) Remind children about the rules. Work as a team to apply a few rules consistently.
___ 2. Toddlers have strong feelings and sometimes express themselves by hitting, pushing, or shoving other children.	(b) Know each child's abilities and personality. Anticipate what he or she might do and intervene when necessary.
___ 3. Following procedures for responding to injuries is one important aspect of a safe program.	(c) Handle minor injuries as needed, complete a report, and inform families at pick up. Know the standard procedures to assess a situation and know when to get immediate medical help.
___ 4. Toddlers are ready to learn a few important safety rules, but you cannot count on their following the rules all of the time.	(d) Make sure the classroom is continuously supervised. Check equipment and materials and remove safety hazards. Watch for and remove broken toys and toys with small parts or sharp edges.
___ 5. Most injuries in an infant toddler program are minor. However, serious illnesses and injuries can also occur.	(e) Know and practice program policies and procedures for responding to injuries and handling emergencies.

Fill in the Blank (5 points each)
Complete each sentence. Number 6 requires two answers, worth a total of 10 points.

6. Two items to be included in a first-aid kit are

    a. _____

    b. _____

7. One important rule to remember when giving first aid is _____

    _____ .

Short Answer (5 points each)

Complete the following exercise. Number 8 requires six answers, worth a total of 30 points.

8. In order to prevent serious injuries, there are things you must never do. For each of the following injuries, give one example of what you must not do.

    a. poisoning

    b. falls and related injuries

    c. choking

    d. strangulation

    e. suffocation

    f. burns

Multiple Choice (5 points each)

Check the response that best completes each sentence.

9. All of the following situations require immediate medical help except

    ☐ a. a child has a seizure
    ☐ b. a child is vomiting blood
    ☐ c. a child has a cut that may require stitches
    ☐ d. a child is unconscious

10. On neighborhood walks

    ☐ a. be sure that each child is in a backpack, stroller, or carriage or holds an adult's hand
    ☐ b. continue to your destination, even if children seem tired
    ☐ c. do not worry about the weather unless it is raining
    ☐ d. make sure children are quiet

Extended Answer (10 points each)

Complete the following exercises.

11. Explain how to help children begin to learn safety practices through everyday experiences.

12. Describe the basic procedures that you would follow if there were an injury or serious illness at the program. Explain how you would assess the situation and determine when and how to seek medical care for a child.

Knowledge Assessment   Module 2: Healthy

You may use Caring for Infants & Toddlers *and your* Skill-Building Journal *to complete this assessment.*

Matching (5 points each)
Choose the lettered item in the right column that best matches each statement in the left column. Write the letter of your choice on the line next to the number of the statement.

___ 1. Germs can be passed from one person to another.	(a) Ill children need additional rest, appropriate food and drinks, close supervision and comfort, and sometimes medication.
___ 2. Children learn good health habits through routines.	(b) Discuss and coordinate the introduction of new foods with families. Introduce one new food at a time. Watch for allergic reactions.
___ 3. Between 4–8 months of age, many infants are ready for solid food.	(c) Follow universal precautions—handwashing, cleaning and disinfecting, and using gloves for contact with blood—to prevent the spread of diseases.
___ 4. Sick children who remain at the center need extra attention.	(d) Use healthy practices. Talk with children about what you do to promote wellness. Use routines as opportunities for health learning.

Fill in the Blank (5 points each)
Complete each sentence. Number 6 requires two answers, worth a total of 10 points.

5. HIV attacks the immune system that protects the body from viruses and bacteria. One way that it can be

   transmitted is by _____.

6. Name two foods that are choking hazards for infants and toddlers.

   a. _____

   b. _____

7. A mandated reporter of possible child abuse and neglect is a person who

   _____.

Short Answer (5 points each)

Complete the following exercises.

8. What is shaken baby syndrome?

9. Explain why teachers wash their own hands and infants' and toddlers' hands thoroughly and frequently.

10. Give a specific example of how health and nutrition learning can be incorporated into a daily routine or activity.

Multiple Choice (5 points each)

Check the response that best completes each sentence.

11. An example of emotional child abuse is

☐ a. when a child is allowed to make choices
☐ b. when a child has a hard time sharing and likes to play alone
☐ c. when a parent teases her child because she is overweight
☐ d. when a child cries because his friend may not come home with him every day

12. A common risk factor for families that can lead to child abuse and neglect is

☐ a. not having two parents living in the same household
☐ b. having children under the age of five
☐ c. children who continually test behavioral limits
☐ d. being under a lot of continuous stress

13. When disinfecting surfaces, toys, and equipment, use all of the following guidelines except

☐ a. use surface bleach solution on a diaper changing station
☐ b. use mild bleach solution for mouthed toys
☐ c. wash and disinfect mouthed toys weekly
☐ d. make fresh bleach solutions daily

14. If there is an outbreak of head lice in your program

    ☐ a. throw out all stuffed animals and pillows
    ☐ b. explain that the children are not bathing often enough
    ☐ c. share information with families about the life cycle of lice and steps that must be taken at home and at the program.
    ☐ d. call a pest control company and make sure that families know the program will be closed when insecticides are sprayed

15. When administering medication

    ☐ a. help families save money by using leftover medication for a child with the same symptoms
    ☐ b. keep all medicine in a locked box in the refrigerator
    ☐ c. make sure that parents give written permission and that you keep accurate records
    ☐ d. give aspirin at the first sign of a cold

Extended Answer (10 points each)

Complete the following exercises.

16. Discuss how teachers promote wellness by sanitizing program spaces. In your answer, include information about what should be cleaned and how.

17. Discuss the key role that teachers play in preventing and stopping child abuse and neglect. In your answer, explain why they are in a position to notice signs of possible abuse and neglect and the importance of reporting what they notice.

Knowledge Assessment	Module 3: Learning Environment

You may use Caring for Infants & Toddlers *and your* Skill-Building Journal *to complete this assessment.*

Matching (5 points each)

Choose the lettered item in the right column that best matches each statement in the left column. Write the letter of your choice on the line next to the number of the statement.

__ 1. Young infants are active explorers who use their senses to learn about the world around them.	(a) Provide a variety of materials to support all areas of development. Include materials typically found at home. Observe how children use materials. Rotate toys that are ignored and add new materials as children's skills and interests change.
__ 2. Mobile infants learn to crawl, walk, and climb. They are eager to explore and investigate everything they can reach. They are developing new fine motor skills.	(b) Respond to children's efforts to communicate and appreciate their growing skills. Respond immediately to children's needs. Share their accomplishments with colleagues and families.
__ 3. Toddlers' cognitive and language skills are growing. They enjoy pretend play. They are refining their fine motor skills.	(c) Help toddlers begin to understand cause and effect and concepts about size, shape, and weight. Provide simple pretend play props and opportunities to use art materials such as paint, playdough, and crayons.
__ 4. Teachers are the most important part of the program environment.	(d) Provide a large, open play area to support gross motor play and exploration. Offer things to stack, fill and dump, push and pull, and fit together.
__ 5. Young children develop and change very quickly. A toy that was challenging last month might seem boring today.	(e) Provide toys that are chewable, washable, and easy to grasp. Offer toys that infants can move or use to make noises.

Fill in the Blank (5 points each)

Complete each sentence. Number 7 requires three answers, worth a total of 15 points.

6. It is recommended that children have at least _____ minutes of outdoor play in the morning and _____ minutes in the afternoon, every day in a full-day program.

7. Three suggestions that a physical or occupational therapist might make to adapt toys and materials for children with special needs are

   a. _____.

   b. _____.

   c. _____.

Short Answer (5 points each)

Complete the following exercises. Number 8 requires four answers, worth a total of 20 points.

8. Give an example of something that a teacher might see a child doing in each of the following classroom areas.

   a. entrance area

   b. indoor play area

   c. outdoor play area

   d. diapering area

Multiple Choice (5 points each)

Check the response that best completes each sentence.

9. Toys and materials for infants and toddlers should meet all of the following criteria except

   ☐ a. related to the children's families, cultures, and home languages
   ☐ b. usable in many different ways
   ☐ c. usable by infants and toddlers only under adult supervision
   ☐ d. encourage children's growth and development

10. An appropriate daily schedule for infants should

   ☐ a. follow each infant's personal schedule for eating, sleeping, diapering, and playing
   ☐ b. limit outdoor time in cold weather
   ☐ c. include time for language drills
   ☐ d. help teachers rush through routines as quickly as possible

11. An ideal outdoor program environment should include

   ☐ a. a nearby pond
   ☐ b. sunny and shady areas
   ☐ c. access from the neighborhood
   ☐ d. a view of the highway

Extended Answer (10 points each)

Complete the following exercises.

12. Explain why it is important to have a consistent but flexible schedule for infants and toddlers.

13. Select a daily routine such as diapering, feeding, or dressing. Give a specific example of small muscle, large muscle, cognitive, and communication skills that a child might be learning during the routine.

Knowledge Assessment	**Module 4: Physical**

You may use Caring for Infants & Toddlers *and your* Skill-Building Journal *to complete this assessment.*

Matching (5 points each)

Choose the lettered item in the right column that best matches each statement in the left column. Write the letter of your choice on the line next to the number of the statement.

___ 1.	To increase their physical abilities, infants and toddlers need gentle challenges that let them practice their physical skills and develop new ones.	(a)	Provide opportunities for infants to participate in daily routines and play, such as picking up food from their plates, turning pages in a book, or taking off their shoes.
___ 2.	As their fine motor skills develop, mobile infants take active roles in routines and play.	(b)	Encourage children of all ages to use physical skills during diapering and toileting. They can climb steps to the diapering table, pull pants up and down, and turn the faucet on. Look for signs of readiness for toilet learning.
___ 3.	Toddlers begin to coordinate eye and hand movements.	(c)	Encourage children to do things such as holding their arms out when you put on their shirt or jacket and taking their shoes off before napping.
___ 4.	Infants and toddlers can practice physical skills while getting dressed and undressed.	(d)	Provide a variety of materials, such as interlocking blocks; pop beads; simple puzzles; and writing, drawing, and painting tools.
___ 5.	Between 24–30 months, children typically become able to control their bladder and bowel muscles.	(e)	Provide indoor and outdoor space so children can move about safely. Provide open-ended materials for children to explore. Observe children engaged in routines and play to find clues about the children's levels of fine and gross motor development.

Fill in the Blank (5 points each)

Complete each sentence. Number 6 requires two answers, worth a total of 10 points. Number 8 requires three answers, worth a total of 15 points.

6. Two adaptations that can be made to encourage the participation of children with physical disabilities are

   a. _____.

   b. _____.

7. The best way to understand how particular children use their fine and gross motor skills is by

   _____.

8. Give three suggestions of what teachers can do to support children's physical development during outdoor play.

a. _____.

b. _____.

c. _____.

Short Answer (5 points each)

Complete the exercise. Number 9 requires three answers, worth a total of 15 points.

9. Explain three specific features of a safe environment that supports physical development.

a.

b.

c.

Multiple Choice (5 points each)

Check the response that best completes each sentence.

10. All of the following are examples of physical developmental alerts except

☐ a. by 4 months, a child does not turn his head to locate sound
☐ b. by 9 months, a child cannot sit up without help or support
☐ c. by 14 months, a child cannot walk
☐ d. by 3 years, a child does not walk down steps

11. To help prevent back injuries,

☐ a. bend from the waist to lift up a baby
☐ b. bend your knees, tuck your buttocks, and pull in your stomach muscles when lifting
☐ c. stand with a child on your hip
☐ d. sit on child-size chairs as often as possible

Extended Answer (10 points each)

Complete the following exercises.

12. Explain how physical development is connected to two other areas of development (cognitive, communication, self, social).

13. Explain the statement, "Physical growth follows a general, predictable pattern."

Knowledge Assessment   Module 5: Cognitive

You may use Caring for Infants & Toddlers *and your* Skill-Building Journal *to complete this assessment.*

Matching (5 points each)
Choose the lettered item in the right column that best matches each statement in the left column. Write the letter of your choice on the line next to the number of the statement.

__ 1. object permanence	(a) materials and toys that children can use in many different ways
__ 2. cause and effect	(b) the process of considering various aspects of a situation and identifying one or more approaches that are likely to lead to solutions
__ 3. cognitive development	(c) the concept that people and things still exist when they are out of sight
__ 4. problem solving	(d) the understanding that a particular action or condition makes something else happen
__ 5. open-ended materials	(e) the process of learning to think and reason

Fill in the Blank (5 points each)
Complete each sentence. Number 7 requires two answers, worth a total of 10 points.

6. One example of how a mobile infant uses an object purposefully is _____

_____.

7. Two examples of toys that react to the actions of infants and toddlers are _____

and _____.

Short Answer (5 points each)

Complete each exercise. Number 8 requires three answers, worth a total of 15 points. Number 9 requires two answers, worth a total of 10 points.

8. Describe one characteristic of young infants, of mobile infants, and of toddlers related to cognitive development.

    a. Young infants

    b. Mobile infants

    c. Toddlers

9. Describe two features of an environment for infants and toddlers that encourage exploration and discovery.

    a.

    b.

Multiple Choice (5 points each)

Check the response that best completes each sentence.

10. All of the following are examples of cognitive development alerts except

    ☐ a. by 5 months, a child does not smile spontaneously
    ☐ b. by 8 months, a child does not show interest in playing peek-a-boo
    ☐ c. by 12 months, a child does not search for objects hidden while he or she watches
    ☐ d. by 2 years, a child cannot copy a circle

11. Toys and materials that support cognitive development

    ☐ a. stimulate children's senses
    ☐ b. are expensive
    ☐ c. break easily
    ☐ d. must be homemade

12. Let children solve problems on their own when

    ☐ a. they are unable to concentrate
    ☐ b. they are in danger
    ☐ c. they are frustrated
    ☐ d. they are focusing and trying different ways to do things

Extended Answer (10 points each)

Complete the following exercises.

13. Select a daily routine and explain how teachers can support children's thinking skills during the routine.

14. Explain how cognitive development is related to two other areas of development (physical, communication, self, social).

Knowledge Assessment	Module 6: Communication

You may use Caring for Infants & Toddlers *and your* Skill-Building Journal *to complete this assessment.*

Matching (5 points each)

Choose the lettered item in the right column that best matches each statement in the left column. Write the letter of your choice on the line next to the number of the statement.

__ 1. Young infants communicate by crying, making other sounds, moving their bodies, and using gestures and facial expressions.	(a) Look at new things together and introduce words to name them. Show excitement when children learn new words.
__ 2. Mobile infants say a few words that refer to people, objects, and actions that interest them.	(b) Try to understand the child's efforts to communicate. Use words to express what the child seems to be saying.
__ 3. Toddlers speak in sentences that gradually increase from two to several words in length.	(c) Provide books that are sturdy and safe for mouthing. Introduce books with textures to feel. Include books with pictures of familiar objects.
__ 4. Infants like to explore the taste and feel of books. They also like to see what is inside.	(d) Provide writing tools, such as chunky crayons, washable markers, and chalk, and provide surfaces to write on, such as big pieces of paper, easels, and blackboards.
__ 5. Toddlers are increasing their eye-hand coordination and small muscle skills.	(e) Restate their sentences to model complete language.

Fill in the Blank (5 points each)

Complete each sentence. Number 6 requires two answers, worth a total of 10 points.

6. Two ways to serve as a language model for infants and toddlers are _____

   _____ and _____

   _____ .

7. *Parentese* is _____ .

8. A *phoneme* is _____ .

Short Answer (5 points each)

Complete the following exercises. Number 9 requires three answers, worth a total of 15 points.

9. Give an example of something to do when reading aloud with toddlers

    a. before you read

    b. during the reading

    c. when you are finished reading

10. Give an example of how communication is connected to one other area of development (cognitive, social/emotional, or physical).

Multiple Choice (5 points each)

Check the response that best completes each sentence.

11. When children are learning one language at home and another in the program

    ☐ a. never use their home languages in the classroom
    ☐ b. encourage their parents to speak only English to their child
    ☐ c. refer a child who is using words from both languages to a speech pathologist
    ☐ d. learn a few important words, phrases, songs, and rhymes in the children's home languages

12. When creating a book area

    ☐ a. keep books out of children's reach so they won't destroy them
    ☐ b. make the area cozy and comfortable
    ☐ c. make sure the book area is the only place in the room where there are books and other print materials
    ☐ d. avoid having any alphabet books in the book area

13. All of the following are examples of language and communication development alerts except by

    ☐ a. 6 months, a child does not notice noisy toys
    ☐ b. 12 months, a child does not say any words, even unclearly
    ☐ c. 18 months, a child does not use two or three word sentences
    ☐ d. 3 years, a child has persistent drooling

Extended Answer (10 points each)

Complete the following exercises.

14. Describe how to set up and use a book area for toddlers.

15. Describe a book that you like to read with a child or children in your group. Think about the developmental characteristics of children that age. Explain why the book is appropriate for children that age.

Knowledge Assessment   Module 7: Creative

You may use Caring for Infants & Toddlers *and your* Skill-Building Journal *to complete this assessment.*

Matching (5 points each)

Choose the lettered item in the right column that best matches each statement in the left column. Write the letter of your choice on the line next to the number of the statement.

___ 1. Young infants use all of their senses to explore the world around them.	(a) Talk about the child's experiences, using words that describe sounds, colors, and textures. Provide beautiful things to look at and touch.
___ 2. Mobile infants are developing fine motor skills.	(b) Sing, move, and dance with children. Provide simple rhythm instruments for them to explore. Introduce a wide variety of musical styles.
___ 3. Toddlers' language skills are expanding rapidly.	(c) Introduce simple art materials and tools such as large crayons, short-handled paint brushes, and dough.
___ 4. Music is an excellent way to promote children's self-expression. Children respond to music at an early age, and they enjoy moving to music.	(d) Share rhymes, songs, fingerplays, and simple stories. Provide realistic dramatic play props related to familiar activities.

Fill in the Blank (5 points each)

Complete each sentence. Number 5 requires two answers, worth a total of 10 points. Number 6 requires three answers, worth a total of 15 points.

5. Two ways to introduce a variety of textures in your classroom are _____

   _____ and _____

   _____.

6. Three characteristics of young children that are linked to creativity are

   a. _____.

   b. _____.

   c. _____.

Short Answer (5 points each)

Complete each exercise. Numbers 7 and 8 each require two answers, so each question is worth a total of 10 points.

7. Give two examples of ways you can provide opportunities for children to make choices.

    a.

    b.

8. Give two examples of ways to encourage creativity throughout the day.

    a.

    b.

9. What is one safety consideration for homemade rattles and shakers?

Multiple Choice (5 points each)

Check the response that best completes each sentence.

10. Music and movement activities encourage self expression and

    ☐ a. help children explore ways to move their bodies
    ☐ b. help teachers get a break during the day
    ☐ c. help teachers learn which children have rhythm
    ☐ d. help children learn the latest dances

11. It is not a good idea to play music
    ☐ a. all of the time
    ☐ b. as a listening activity
    ☐ c. of a variety of styles and cultures
    ☐ d. to signal a transition

Extended Answer (10 points each)

Complete the following exercises.

12. Describe one basic art experience that is appropriate for mobile infants and toddlers. Explain why it is appropriate. Give examples of materials and tools to provide. Note two special considerations.

13. Describe how to introduce fingerplays to infants and toddlers, and explain how infants and toddlers might participate.

Knowledge Assessment   Module 8: Self

You may use Caring for Infants and Toddlers *and your* Skill-Building Journal *to complete this assessment.*

Matching (5 points each)

Choose the lettered item in the right column that best matches each statement in the left column. Write the letter of your choice on the line next to the number of the statement.

__ 1. sense of self	(a) The concept that people and things still exist when they are out of sight.
__ 2. social development	(b) A sense of worth; a feeling about one's abilities and accomplishments.
__ 3. separation anxiety	(c) The gradual process through which children learn to enjoy being with other people and eventually gain skills such as sharing, cooperating, negotiating, and empathizing.
__ 4. object permanence	(d) A preference for being with people whom infants and toddlers know well; dislike of being around new people. May be expressed as difficulty saying goodbye to family members. Typically occurs at about 8 months of age and sometimes again at around 18 months.
__ 5. self-esteem	(e) Understanding who you are; how you identify yourself in terms of culture, environment, physical attributes, preferences, skills, and experiences.

Fill in the Blank (5 points each)

Complete each sentence.

6. The best way to help infants build a sense of trust is to _____

    _____.

7. One reason that toddlers say *no* and use the *m* words *me*, *my*, and *mine* is _____

    _____.

8. It is important to repeat activities so that infants and toddlers _____

    _____.

9. It is important for teachers to know when to offer a child help and when to _____

    _____.

10. It is also important for teachers to talk with children about their families during the day because _____

    _____.

Short Answer (5 points each)

Complete the following exercises. Number 12 requires two answers, worth a total of 10 points..

11. Give a brief example of language that helps a child feel valued and respected.

12. When you acknowledge a child's effort or accomplishment, you want express yourself in a way that is meaningful and useful to the child. Describe two things to include in your acknowledgment when you talk with the child.

    a.

    b.

Multiple Choice (5 points each)

Check the response that best completes each sentence.

13. When a child has an toileting accident

    ☐ a. make sure the parents know that their child soiled his clothing
    ☐ b. respond matter-of-factly and reassure the child that toileting accidents sometimes happen
    ☐ c. stop toilet learning immediately and wait until the child is ready
    ☐ d. remind the child that having a toileting accident is "yucky"

14. All of the following are good ways to support daily separation from families except

    ☐ a. making sure that families leave as quickly and quietly as possible
    ☐ b. establishing a goodbye ritual
    ☐ c. including family photos in the room
    ☐ d. encouraging families to bring their child's comfort items from home

15. Children sometimes cry when they see their families at the end of the day because

    ☐ a. they are busy and don't want to go home
    ☐ b. they are afraid of the family pets
    ☐ c. they can no longer hold back their feelings about missing their parents all day
    ☐ d. they are hungry and ready for dinner

Extended Answer (10 points each)

Complete the following exercises.

16. Describe signs that a child is ready, willing, and able to learn to use the toilet.

17. Name Eric Erikson's first two stages of social/emotional development and describe what teachers can do to support children in each of the stages.

Knowledge Assessment — Module 9: Social

You may use Caring for Infants & Toddlers *and your* Skill-Building Journal *to complete this assessment.*

Matching (5 points each)

Choose the lettered item in the right column that best matches each statement in the left column. Write the letter of your choice on the line next to the number of the statement.

___ 1. Young infants learn to enjoy being with people. They show a preference for human faces and voices.	(a) Help children identify and name their feelings, and help them learn to cope with feelings without being aggressive toward people or things.
___ 2. Mobile infants learn social skills through their relationships with their families and teachers.	(b) Provide an open-ended environment and activities in which friendships are likely to flourish. Stay nearby and observe, but only step in when needed.
___ 3. Toddlers have strong, sometimes conflicting feelings and often do not know how to express them.	(c) Provide loving, consistent care. Talk and play with them so they can experience the joy of human relationships.
___ 4. Children develop social skills by having opportunities to play with familiar peers who like to do the same things.	(d) Play games and read with them. Begin to teach them to help and comfort others.

Fill in the Blank (5 points each)

Complete each sentence.

5. The ongoing, mutual relationship between infants and their primary caregivers, developed gradually during the first year of life when children receive consistent, dependable, and responsive care is called

   _____.

6. _____ is the ability to give to others.

7. The most direct way for infants and toddlers to learn caring behaviors is _____

   _____.

8. The ability to recognize and identify with another person's feelings, thoughts, and experiences is called

   _____.

9. The gradual process through which children learn to enjoy being with other people and gain skills such as

   sharing, cooperating, and empathizing is called _____.

Short Answer (5 points each)

Complete the following exercises. Number 11 requires four answers, worth a total of 20 points.

10. Define *interdependence* and briefly explain why it is important.

11. Give an example of how social development is connected to each of the following aspects of development

    a. physical development

    b. cognitive development

    c. communication (language development)

    d. emotional development

Multiple Choice (5 points each)

Check the response that best completes each sentence.

12. All of the following are examples of social development alerts for infants and toddlers except

    ☐ a. by 5 months, a child does not smile spontaneously
    ☐ b. by 8 months, a child does not follow simple instructions
    ☐ c. by 12 months, a child does not imitate actions or words
    ☐ d. by 3 years, a child does not engage in pretend play

13. The most important part of an infant or toddler environment is

    ☐ a. the caregiver
    ☐ b. the diaper-changing table
    ☐ c. a quiet space for children to be alone
    ☐ d. an outdoor area

Extended Answer (10 points each)

Complete the following exercises.

14. Explain why it is important to create places for infants and toddlers to be alone when they want to be. Also describe two ideas for creating quiet places.

15. Explain why it is important to include items like those in the children's homes and describe two ways to achieve a homelike setting.

Knowledge Assessment		**Module 10: Guidance**

You may use Caring for Infants & Toddlers *and your* Skill-Building Journal *to complete this assessment.*

Matching (5 points each)

Choose the lettered item in the right column that best matches each statement in the left column. Write the letter of your choice on the line next to the number of the statement.

__ 1. Young infants cry to express physical discomfort, boredom, stress, and frustration. They cry to let adults know when they need something.	(a) Respond promptly to their cries. When their needs are met promptly and consistently, they learn to tolerate short waits to have their needs met. This is the beginning of self-control.
__ 2. Like young infants and toddlers, mobile infants are interested in other children.	(b) Set clear and consistent limits. Provide frequent reminders of which behaviors are acceptable and which are not.
__ 3. Toddlers are learning which behaviors are acceptable and which are not, but they are not always able to stop themselves from doing something that is not allowed.	(c) Regularly exchange information with families about how their children are developing and learning. Describe both positive and unwanted behaviors, and discuss strategies to support the child. Address the behavior as challenging, not the child.
__ 4. It is best for teachers and families to work together to help children with problem behavior.	(d) Use your knowledge of typical child development to understand the behavior of individual children. Think about what might be causing particular behaviors.
__ 5. Children behave inappropriately for a variety of reasons.	(e) Play with two children at the same time. Show them how to enjoy being together and how to touch others gently.

Fill in the Blank (5 points each)

Complete each sentence.

6. The ability to manage feelings and control actions is called _____.

7. Our _____ affects how we respond to environments, people, and experiences throughout life.

8. A good time to use the word _____ is to prevent a child from harming himself or someone else.

Short Answer (5 points each)

Complete the following exercises. Number 11 requires three answers, worth a total of 15 points.

9. Give one reason a toddler might bite that is not an example of aggression.

10. Give an example of a way to provide toddlers with opportunities to say *no* without causing problems.

11. Give an example of an unwanted behavior and suggest three reasons why a child might behave in that way.

    a.

    b.

    c.

12. Describe what sometimes happens when a child is about to reach a major milestone, or "touchpoint."

Multiple Choice (5 points each)

Check the response that best completes each sentence.

13. An example of an acceptable choice to offer a mobile infant or toddler is

    ☐ a. It's time to change your wet shirt. Do you want to put on your blue shirt or your red shirt?
    ☐ b. We're going outside. Do you want to come with us or stay inside by yourself?
    ☐ c. Do you want to paint the wall or the paper?
    ☐ d. We're going to cross the street. Do you want to hold my hand or walk across like a big boy?

14. It is difficult for toddlers to share and take turns. It is therefore a good idea to

    ☐ a. put all the toys away until toddlers are ready to share
    ☐ b. give each child five minutes to play with a favorite toy
    ☐ c. have multiples of popular items
    ☐ d. ask toddlers to bring in toys from home to share in the program

Extended Answer (10 points each)

Complete the following exercises.

15. Select one aspect of temperament and describe behaviors that two very different children might exhibit in relation to that trait.

16. Briefly discuss the seven steps to follow in preventing and responding to problem behavior.

Knowledge Assessment   Module 11: Families

You may use Caring for Infants & Toddlers *and your* Skill-Building Journal *to complete this assessment.*

Matching (5 points each)

Choose the lettered item in the right column that best matches each statement in the left column. Write the letter of your choice on the line next to the number of the statement.

___ 1. Partnerships between families and teachers are extremely important for everyone. Children feel secure, knowing that their families and teachers work together to keep them safe and help them learn.	(a) Explain to families the importance of letting children know when they are leaving the program and of assuring the children that they will return to pick them up.
___ 2. Separation difficulties are stressful for children and families. Teachers can provide guidance to help them with the separation process.	(b) Invite families to be part of the program's activities. Invite families to visit or to help in the classroom, come along on trips, share special events, and contribute to supplies and projects.
___ 3. Keeping families informed is crucial to successful partnerships between families and the program. Teachers use many approaches to exchange information with families.	(c) Hold conferences throughout the year and make sure families know they can ask for a conference whenever they want to exchange information. Keep families informed daily and throughout the year about how their children are developing and learning.
___ 4. Most families want to be involved in their children's lives in the program. Family involvement and support can be an important resource for the program.	(d) Get to know a little about each family. Communicate frequently to share information and offer a variety of ways for families to participate in the program. Plan and hold conferences, and provide support to families in a variety of ways.
___ 5. Conferences are opportunities for teachers to focus on one child and family. Through conferences, families and teachers share information about how best to support an individual child's development and learning.	(e) Find ways to communicate with families regularly. Ask families which methods would be most useful to them. Use newsletters, e-mail, conferences, special events, phone calls, and informal conversations to keep families informed about their children and the program.

Fill in the Blank (5 points each)

Complete each sentence.

6. In addition to sharing information about their children, families can share _____

_____.

7. Families should not leave the classroom without saying _____ to their children.

8. One method that can be used to communicate with families is _____.

9. Teachers should be aware of _____ differences that need to be recognized and respected.

Short Answer (5 points each)

Complete the following exercises.

10. Explain what is meant by the term *maintaining confidentiality*.

11. Give one example of information a teacher will want to learn from the family during a conference.

12. Give one example of information a family will want to learn from the teacher during a conference.

13. Give one example of a source of long-term family stress.

14. Give one example of how teachers help families find resources or get more information about a topic that interests them.

Multiple Choice (5 points each)

Check the response that best completes each sentence.

15. A way teachers can make family conferences successful is to

☐ a. give families a lot of materials to read and study ahead of time
☐ b. repeat what they think they have heard, to make sure they understand what a family member said
☐ c. make sure families arrive on time
☐ d. hold conferences early in the morning when everyone is fresh

16. If there is a conflict between the program and a family's expectations, a teacher may want to

☐ a. ask the program director to request the family's cooperation
☐ b. tell the family that the program has specific guidelines they must follow
☐ c. ignore the problem until the parent finally accepts the program's practices
☐ d. try to understand the family's view and jointly determine a solution

Extended Answer (10 points each)

Complete the following exercises.

17. Explain how you would prepare for a conference with a family. Discuss your ideas about scheduling the conference, as well as the information you would want to gather.

18. Describe one way to involve families in a specific activity. Also explain two strategies that help ensure that the families' participation is meaningful for them.

Knowledge Assessment   Module 12: Program Management

You may use Caring for Infants and Toddlers *and your* Skill-Building Journal *to complete this assessment.*

Matching (5 points each)

Choose the lettered item in the right column that best matches each statement in the left column. Write the letter of your choice on the line next to the number of the statement.

___ 1. Program management includes creating a supportive learning environment, guiding children's learning, and assessing children's progress. Knowledge of children's developmental and individual characteristics guides program planning and implementation.	(a) Provide activities that accommodate the varying skills, interests, and abilities of all children. Make changes or adjustments for individual children, as needed for them to participate in all parts of the program. Make inclusion an integral part of the program's environment and practice.
___ 2. A portfolio includes items that document a child's growth and development. It is an excellent way to document a child's progress over time.	(b) High-quality programs are based on child development principles and theory, and they are tailored to correspond with the characteristics of individual children. Work as a team to plan and implement a responsive program. Appreciate and use the strengths of all team members, including teachers, families, and volunteers.
___ 3. Individual needs can be met during group activities, as well as by working with children one-on-one.	(c) Throughout the year, collect items such as photographs, observation notes, and notes from parents. Document and keep observation notes about what children do. Organize examples that show how the children learn and are progressing. Invite families to contribute and share the collection with family members.
___ 4. High-quality programs ensure that every child can learn and succeed. An environment that supports inclusion of children with disabilities and different needs helps all children to thrive.	(d) Learn what makes each child special. Vary teaching strategies to respond to each child during regular program activities. Offer encouragement and build on each child's skills and interests.

Fill in the Blank (5 points each)

Complete each sentence. Numbers 6 and 7 each require two answers, so each question is worth a total of 10 points.

5. Useful observation notes are complete, accurate, and_____.

6. A program should have a written _____ to guide teachers' work and an

    _____ to determine how each child is progressing.

7. Two reasons why teachers observe children are

    a. _____.

    b. _____.

8. It is important to observe children in different settings and at different times of the day because

_____

_____.

Short Answer (5 points each)

Complete the following exercises. Number 10 requires two answers, worth a total of 10 points.

9. Give an example of an item that could be included in a child's portfolio.

10. List at least two good sources of information about a child with a disability.

a.

b.

11. Describe one item that should be included in a weekly planning discussion.

Multiple Choice (5 points each)

Check the response that best completes each sentence.

12. The following is an objective and accurate description of a child engaged in an activity:

☐ a. Luis hurried to get a tricycle, anxious to get it before Britney. He fell, got up, and began whining. He went over to Mrs. Marker.
☐ b. Luis hurried to the tricycle but fell. He started crying because his leg hurt, and he limped to Mrs. Marker.
☐ c. Luis was on the swings. He walked to the tricycle but fell. He got up, started crying, and limped to Mrs. Marker.
☐ d. Luis hurried to get a tricycle. On the way, he fell down and seemed to hurt his leg. He got up and cried in pain. He went directly to Mrs. Marker.

13. The following would be a good item to include in a child's portfolio

☐ a. a note the parent sent to the teacher about a minor injury
☐ b. a photograph of the child's fingerpainting
☐ c. a copy of the daily schedule
☐ d. a photograph of the child's cubby

Extended Answer (10 points each)

Complete the following exercises.

14. Discuss the kinds of questions that teachers ask when evaluating the program at the end of each day.

15. Explain why a team approach to program planning and evaluation is useful.

Knowledge Assessment — Module 13: Professionalism

You may use Caring for Infants & Toddlers *and your* Skill-Building Journal *to complete this assessment.*

Matching (5 points each)

Choose the lettered item in the right column that best matches each statement in the left column. Write the letter of your choice on the line next to the number of the statement.

___ 1. Professional standards guide practice in the early childhood field. Standards define both teacher competence and program quality.	(a) Regularly take advantage of professional development opportunities, such as training workshops and conferences. Learn about current issues and policies in the early childhood field by reading and talking with families and colleagues.
___ 2. Teachers continue to grow professionally as they gain experience and refine their skills. It is important for teachers to continue to learn and to keep up-to-date about developmentally appropriate practices.	(b) When a difficult situation arises, consult the NAEYC *Code of Ethical Conduct* for guidance on resolving the problem. Be familiar with your program's philosophy and policies, including those regarding conflicts. Regularly attend staff meetings to discuss standards, concerns, and ways to resolve problems.
___ 3. A code of ethics provides educators with guidelines for acting responsibly and for resolving difficult problems in ways that balance the needs of children, families, and colleagues.	(c) Act on behalf of all children. Share positive experiences and strategies for promoting children's growth and development with families. Stay current with early childhood policies and pending legislation. Become involved on a state and/or national level.
___ 4. An advocate is someone who works for a cause. It is important to share what you know about the needs of young children and about what helps them learn and thrive.	(d) Become familiar with the guidelines for the early childhood field. Make sure you understand developmentally appropriate practice and what expectations and limits are reasonable for the children in your care.

Fill in the Blank (5 points each)

Complete each sentence.

5. A professional is a person who has specialized _____ and

   _____.

6. Advocacy means working for _____.

7. NAEYC issues position statements in order to _____

   _____.

8. Lilian Katz identifies four stages in teaching: survival, consolidation, renewal, and maturity. A teacher at the survival stage would be concerned about _____

_____.

9. One ethical responsibility that early childhood professionals have to their co-workers is _____

_____.

Short Answer (5 points each)

Complete the following exercises. Number 10 requires two answers, worth a total of 10 points.

10. Identify two ways that teachers can continue to grow and learn professionally.

   a.

   b.

11. Explain one of the ways teachers can advocate for children and early childhood programs.

12. Name one early childhood professional organization and describe the resources it provides.

13. Give a brief example of how teachers uphold the ethic of treating families respectfully, even in difficult situations.

Multiple Choice (5 points each)

Check the response that best completes each sentence.

14. The following is an example of professional behavior

   ☐ a. having all children participate in the same activities at the same time
   ☐ b. making the effort to understand why a child is misbehaving
   ☐ c. talking about a particular child's behavior with another child's parent
   ☐ d. making sure that all the children know how to walk in a straight line

15. Mature teachers are

    ☐ a. over the age of 55
    ☐ b. teachers who have taught for 20 years or more
    ☐ c. teachers who realize that children can be expected to work, not play
    ☐ d. committed professionals who continually seek new ideas, skills, and challenges

Extended Answer (10 points each)

Complete the following exercises.

16. Explain why you should talk about the value of your work.

17. Think about strategies that early childhood educators can use to continue learning. Choose two strategies that you have found effective and explain why they were useful.

Knowledge Assessment   Answer Sheets

The Knowledge Assessment *for each module is worth a total of 100 points when all questions are answered correctly. A score of 80 points or more is needed to pass the* Knowledge Assessment *for any module. The questions are scored as follows:*

Matching – 5 points each

Fill in the Blank – 5 points for each required answer. Some questions require more than one answer.

Short Answers – 5 points for each required answer. Some questions require more than one answer.

Extended Answer – 10 points each

Module 1: Safe

Matching

1. d

2. b

3. e

4. a

5. c

Fill in the Blank

6. The contents of a basic first-aid kit are listed on page 25 of *Caring for Infants & Toddlers*. Some examples are nonstick gauze pads, eye dressing, cold pack, emergency contact information, and first aid guide. Accept any items that are included in the list.

7. Answers should include one of the following two rules to remember when giving first aid: 1) do no harm and 2) do not move a child who may have a head, neck, or back injury.

Short Answer

8. There are many correct answers. The chart on page 18 of *Caring for Infants & Toddlers* gives examples of dangerous practices. Accept one example from the chart for each of the following: poisoning, falls and injuries, choking, strangulation, suffocation, and burns.

Multiple Choice

9. c

10. a

Extended Answer

11. Ways to introduce safety practices to children are discussed on pages 29–32 of *Caring for Infants & Toddlers*. Answers should include at least three strategies. Here are some examples:

    • Model good safety habits.

    • Show infants and toddlers how to take steps to prevent injuries, such as putting away broken toys until they can be mended.

    • Talk to the children about what the teachers are doing to prevent injuries.

    • Introduce a few simple and important safety rules to toddlers, but do not expect them to follow the rules all of the time.

12. These are the steps to follow to assess an emergency situation:

    a. Find out what happened.

    b. Check for life-threatening problems using the ABCs (open the airway, check for breathing, check for circulation.

    c. Call emergency medical services (911 or an ambulance) if the child's condition is serious.

    d. Check for injuries, starting at the head and working down.

    e. Calm the other children.

    f. Contact the child's parents or guardians as soon as possible.

    g. Follow the program's procedures for filing an injury/incident report.

Module 2: Healthy

Matching

1. c

2. d

3. b

4. a

Fill in the Blank

5. HIV can be transmitted from mother to child during pregnancy or delivery, through sexual intercourse, by sharing or being stuck with intravenous needles that contain infected blood from a previous user, and from blood and blood product transfusions before 1985. Answers only need to include one of these means of transmission.

6. Answers should include two foods that can cause choking. Examples include large pieces of raw carrots, hot dog chunks, popcorn, nuts, whole grapes, and spoonfuls of peanut butter.

7. Mandated reporters are persons who are required by law to report suspected child abuse and neglect.

Short Answer

8. Shaken baby syndrome results when an adult violently shakes an infant or young child. This can cause hemorrhaging of the brain and eyes and lead to mental retardation, blindness, deafness, and even death.

9. Teachers wash their own hands and help as children wash their hands in order to minimize the spread of infection, to model healthy practice, and to promote children's self-help skills.

10. There are many correct answers. Suggestions for introducing health and nutrition throughout the day are provided on pages 69–73 of *Caring for Infants & Toddlers*. Answers do not need to be extensive.

Multiple Choice

11. c

12. d

13. c

14. c

15. c

Extended Answer

16. Sanitizing surfaces, toys, and equipment; maintaining bathrooms; hygienic food practices; and promoting wellness while children sleep at the center are discussed on pages 48–58 and 65–68 of *Caring for Infants & Toddlers*. Answers should address all classroom areas, not simply toys and tables.

17. Teachers play two key roles in preventing and stopping child abuse and neglect. First, because they care for children daily, they may notice signs of possible abuse and neglect that otherwise might go unnoticed. Second, all states require teachers to report their suspicions of abuse and neglect in accordance with state and local laws. In addition, teachers have an ethical and professional responsibility to keep children safe and to know and follow the reporting requirements and procedures of their state, community, and program. They are also in a position to develop relationships with families and to offer support when it is needed.

Module 3: Learning Environment

Matching

1. e

2. d

3. c

4. b

5. a

Fill in the Blank

6. It is recommended that, in full-day programs, children play outdoors twice a day for 30–45 minutes each time (unless the weather is severe).

7. Examples of suggestions that a physical or occupational therapist might make to adapt toys and materials for children with special needs are provided on page 109 of *Caring for Infants & Toddlers*.

Short Answer

8. There many correct answers. Examples of what a teacher might observe in the entrance area are on page 100 of *Caring for Infants & Toddlers*. Examples of what a teacher might observe in the play area are on pages 102–103. Examples of what a teacher might observe in the outdoor play area are on pages 104–105, and examples for the diapering area are on pages 101–102.

Multiple Choice

9. c

10. a

11. b

Extended Answer

12. A consistent schedule helps infants and toddlers learn that their world is predictable. It also gives families an idea of what takes place each day. However, the schedule must also be flexible so that teachers can meet the needs of individual children. Infants follow a personal schedule for eating, sleeping, diapering, and playing. A flexible schedule for toddlers allows teachers to turn an unplanned activity into a "teachable moment," i.e., into a learning opportunity for the children.

13. There are many correct answers, but teachers should mention that daily routines provide opportunities for children to develop small muscle, large muscle, social, language, and cognitive skills. They should provide a specific example for each.

Module 4: Physical

Matching

1. e

2. a

3. d

4. c

5. b

Fill in the Blank

6. Examples of adaptations that can be made to encourage the participation of children with physical disabilities include providing adaptive equipment and specially designed furniture; positioning children with cushions, bolsters, and wedges so that they can reach materials that are otherwise inaccessible, and gluing corks and large wooden beads to puzzle pieces and other toys to make them easier to grasp. Accept any three reasonable adaptations.

7. The best way to understand how particular children use their fine and gross motor skills is by observing them.

Short Answer

8. There are many acceptable answers, but they must include three suggestions. Here are some key ideas:

    a. Pay attention to what the children are doing and participate with them.

    b. Position yourself at the children's level whenever possible.

    c. Coordinate with colleagues to schedule short breaks so that you can model stretching or taking a quick run around the yard.

    Any other reasonable suggestion is also acceptable.

9. There are many correct answers. Specific features of a safe environment that support physical development are discussed on pages 134–136 of *Caring for Infants & Toddlers*. Accept any three examples that include an explanation.

Multiple Choice

10. c

11. b

Extended Answer

12. There are many correct answers. Connections between physical development and other types of development are discussed on page 132 of *Caring for Infants & Toddlers*.

13. For most children, large muscle control begins with the head and progresses to the legs and feet. Physical development typically starts with the center of the body and moves outward to the fingers and toes. Skills involving the large muscles in a child's arms and legs develop before fine motor skills.

    Answers that instead address the difference between typical development (general developmental pattern of and expectations for an age group) and individual development (the developmental pattern of and expectations for a particular child) are also acceptable.

Module 5: Cognitive

Matching

1. c

2. d

3. e

4. b

5. a

Fill in the Blank

6. Accept any answer that shows the use of an object for a purpose. One example is tugging on a string to bring a toy closer. Another is stacking several small blocks to make a tower.

7. Many toys and materials are affected by the actions of infants and toddlers. Answers should include at least two examples. Some examples are bat-and-kick crib toys; grasp-and-shake rattles; toys that make noise; jack-in-the-boxes and other pop-up toys; and toys with dials, knobs, and push-buttons. When toddlers play with art materials, sand and water props, musical instruments, or toys and games, they also are experimenting with materials that are affected by their actions.

Short Answer

8. There are many acceptable answers. The chart, "Development of Infants and Toddlers," on page 162 of *Caring for Infants & Toddlers* lists characteristics of infants and toddlers related to cognitive development.

9. To allow children to explore freely, the environment must be safe. The environment should be filled with interesting objects for children to manipulate. It should also include areas for moving, so that children can use their senses and motor skills. The environment must also include caring adults who respond and talk to children. Correct answers should include two features.

Multiple Choice

10. d

11. a

12. d

Extended Answer

13. There are many acceptable answers. Pages 170–171 of *Caring for Infants & Toddlers* provides information about how teachers can promote cognitive development during diapering, while feeding infants, and while preparing and eating meals and snacks with older children. Answers should emphasize engaging with and responding to children during daily routines in order to help them construct understandings about the world.

14. Explanations of how cognitive development is related to development in other domains are provided on page 163 of *Caring for Infants & Toddlers*. Answers should include two other areas of development.

Module 6: Communication

Matching

1. b

2. a

3. e

4. c

5. d

Fill in the Blank

6. Suggestions for serving as a language model are provided on pages 200–201 of *Caring for Infants & Toddlers*. Accept any two of the suggestions or other reasonable answers.

7. *Parentese* is the exaggerated, drawn-out speech that many adults use when talking to babies. It is characterized by a slow tempo, simple vocabulary, repeated questions, melodic pitch, and sing-song rhythm.

8. *Phonemes* are the distinctive sounds that make up a language. They are the sounds that are used to form words.

Short Answer

9. Tips for reading aloud with toddlers are provided on page 210 of *Caring for Infants & Toddlers*. Answers only need to include one example for each time period.

10. There are many possible answers. Examples of how communication is connected to other areas of development are provided on page 191 of *Caring for Infants & Toddlers*.

Multiple Choice

11. d

12. b

13. c

Extended Answer

14. Set up a book area in a quiet corner of the room, out of the way of traffic and noisy activities. Make the area comfortable. Display books so that children can see and reach them easily. Provide good lighting. Add dolls and stuffed animals for children to cuddle. Spend time in the book area, and read with children individually or in very small groups.

15. The characteristics of good books for infants and toddlers are discussed on pages 203–206 of *Caring for Infants & Toddlers*. Answers should explain how the characteristics of the selected book correspond with the skills, interests, and needs of the children in the teacher's group.

Module 7: Creative

Matching

1. a

2. c

3. d

4. b

Fill in the Blank

5. Four tips for providing a variety of textures are provided on page 235 of *Caring for Infants & Toddlers*. They include these suggestions:

   • Offer books of different textures.

   • Collect fabric scraps of different textures.

   • Stitch ribbon scraps to fabric.

   • Scatter carpet samples and thick fabric scraps where infants can crawl to or over them safely.

   Accept any two of these ideas as well as other answers that reflect an understanding of how to encourage infants and toddlers to explore a variety of textures.

6. The three key characteristics are a) learning through their senses and paying close attention to the sight, sound, taste, smell, and feel of things around them; b) eagerness to experiment and test ideas and lack of inhibition; and c) absorption in an engaging activity and ability to stay involved as long as their interest lasts. Answers do not need to be exhaustive. Other acceptable answers include characteristics such as having vivid imaginations, curiosity, increasing ability to solve problems, increasing ability to manipulate tools and materials, ability to gather and use information, increasing ability to use language.

Short Answer

7. Teachers can provide opportunities for children to make choices by letting them decide which toys they want to play with, letting them use open-ended materials in a variety of ways, offering choices of snacks, and letting children figure out how to do things for themselves. Other acceptable answers include such strategies as letting children decide with whom to play, what color shirt to wear, and which story to hear. Accept examples of children making simple, safe choices. Answers do not need to be exhaustive.

8. *Caring for Infants & Toddlers* discusses five ways to encourage creativity throughout the day:

   - Provide materials for children to make discoveries.

   - Promote safe exploration.

   - Allow plenty of time and support for children to help with everyday tasks.

   - Talk and sing with children.

   - Prompt children's creative thinking.

   Answers should include two of the five possibilities listed above. Accept other answers that encourage children to explore and experiment; try new ways of doing something; learn from a mistake; respond to art, music, and language; express feelings; and so on.

9. Homemade rattles and shakers must be tightly secured and inspected regularly to make sure that children cannot reach the small pieces that are inside.

Multiple Choice

10. a

11. a

Extended Answer

12. The five basic art experiences detailed on pages 238–240 of *Caring for Infants & Toddlers* are painting, fingerpainting, drawing, tearing and pasting, and playing with dough. Answers should include a reason why the activity is appropriate for infants and toddlers, examples of materials and tools, and two special considerations. Special considerations are noted for each activity.

13. Infants and toddlers enjoy listening to and watching fingerplays. They may try to imitate the movements, but most will probably not be able to coordinate their fingers or sing or say the words. A teacher can introduce fingerplays to a child by placing the child on her lap, or to a small group of children by sitting with them on the floor. The children should face the teacher. Children will participate in different ways, ranging from laughing and smiling to singing and imitating some of the movements.

Module 8: Self

Matching

1. e

2. c

3. d

4. a

5. b

Fill in the Blank

6. The best way to help children develop a sense of trust is to meet their basic needs promptly, consistently, and with care.

7. Toddlers say *no* and use the *m* words *me*, *my*, and *mine* to show that they are becoming independent. Accept answers that reflect an understanding that developing autonomy is a stage of toddler development and that toddlers are asserting their growing independence, not simply misbehaving.

8. It is important to repeat activities so that infants and toddlers can practice and master skills and experience success.

9. It is important for teachers to know when to offer help and when gradually to withdraw support so the child can manage independently. Any answer is acceptable that articulates teachers' need to judge when intervention and direction is appropriate and when to stand back so a child can experience the pleasure of working independently. Teachers should tailor their support to meet the needs of individual children in different situations.

10. It is important for teachers to talk with children about their families during the day because it helps children feel connected to their families and tells children that teachers think their families are important.

Short Answer

11. Examples of caring language are provided on page 258 of *Caring for Infants & Toddlers*. Accept answers that show that teachers enjoy being with children, pay attention to children and notice what they do, observe to see what children need, and help meet children's needs.

12. A meaningful and useful acknowledgment is specific. It describes the child's actions and explains why they are appreciated. Vague, general statements such as "Good job" do not have much value.

Multiple Choice

13. b

14. a

15. c

Extended Answer

16. *Learning Activity D*, module 8, *Caring for Infants & Toddlers* focuses on supporting toddlers during toilet learning. The chart on page 265 and the text on page 266 include signs that a child is ready, willing, and able to start toilet learning.

17. Erikson's first two stages of social/emotional development are discussed on page 252 of *Caring for Infants & Toddlers*. Answers should include a brief description of what teachers can do to support children in each stage.

Module 9: Social

Matching

1. c

2. d

3. a

4. b

Fill in the Blank

5. The ongoing, mutual relationship between infants and their primary caregivers, developed gradually during the first year of life when children receive consistent, dependable, and responsive care is called *attachment*.

6. Generosity is the ability to give to others.

7. The most direct way for infants and toddlers to begin learning caring behaviors is by watching the adults who care for them.

8. The ability to recognize and identify with another person's feelings is called *empathy*.

9. The gradual process through which children learn to enjoy being with other people and gain skills such as sharing, cooperating, and empathizing is called *social development*.

Short Answer

10. Interdependence is the understanding that we are all connected with each other and need to live cooperatively. In the United States, great emphasis is placed on independence, but interdependence is highly valued in many cultures. It is important for children to learn to do things on their own, but it is equally important for children to learn to value relationships and care about others. Answers need not be extensive, but they should reflect an understanding that interdependence is as important as independence.

11. The ways in which social development is connected to other aspects of development are described on page 283 of *Caring for Infants & Toddlers*. There are many correct answers. Answers should include a specific example of physical, cognitive, communication/language, and emotional development.

Multiple Choice

12. b

13. a

Extended Answer

14. Spending a whole day in a group setting can be stressful for both children and adults. Infants and toddlers need places where they can be alone for a while and places where they can watch what is going on around them, as well as small places where two or three children can play. Many ideas for providing quiet places are described on page 286 of *Caring for Infants & Toddlers*. Also accept other creative ideas for quiet places.

15. A homelike setting helps infants and toddlers feel comfortable, secure, and connected to their families during the day. Page 287 of *Caring for Infants & Toddlers* describes several ways to include family photos in the room, and page 288 gives ideas for other homelike touches.

Module 10: Guidance

Matching

1. a

2. e

3. b

4. c

5. d

Fill in the Blank

6. The ability to manage feelings and control actions is called *self-control*.

7. Our temperament affects how we respond to environments, people, and experiences throughout life.

8. Use the word *no* to prevent a child from harming himself or someone else. *Stop* and other words that directly tell a child not to do something are also acceptable answers.

Short Answer

9. There are several reasons why infants and toddlers bite that are not aggressive. They are discussed on pages 323–324 of *Caring for Infants & Toddlers*. Answers need not be extensive, but they should include one specific example of a non-aggressive reason why infants and toddlers sometimes bite.

10. One way to give toddlers an acceptable way to practice saying *no* is to ask silly questions, such as "Do we swim in the snow?" Any other reasonable answer is also acceptable.

11. Possible causes for a child's problem behavior are listed on pages 320 and 322–324 of *Caring for Infants & Toddler*s. Answers should include three causes that might be reasonable explanations for the identified behavior.

12. When a child is about to reach a major milestone, or "touchpoint," he or she may return to behavior used when younger, get upset easily, or behave in an unwanted way.

Multiple Choice

13. a

14. c

Extended Answer

15. Aspects of temperament are discussed on pages 311–313 of *Caring for Infants & Toddlers*. Answers should include one of the four traits discussed (intensity, activity level, persistence, or coping with change) and include an example of a high- and a low-range behavior in relation to the trait.

16. The seven steps to use in preventing and responding to typical problem behaviors are described on page 321 of *Caring for Infants & Toddlers*.

Module 11: Families

Matching

1. d

2. a

3. e

4. b

5. c

Fill in the Blank

6. Families can share their talents, interests, energy, resources, cultures, and so on.

7. Families should not leave the classroom without saying goodbye to their children.

8. Pages 338–339 of *Caring for Infants & Toddlers* offer many suggestions of ways to communicate with families. Answers do not need to be extensive.

9. Teachers should be aware of cultural differences that need to be recognized and respected.

Short Answer

10. *Maintaining confidentiality* means that private information about a person or family will only be shared with persons who have a professional need to know the information.

11. Information that families can offer about their children during a conference is discussed on page 336 of *Caring for Infants & Toddlers*. Answers only need to include one type of information.

12. Information that teachers can offer about a child during a conference is discussed on page 337 of *Caring for Infants & Toddlers*. Answers only need to include one type of information.

13. Sources of long-term stress are listed on page 357 of *Caring for Infants & Toddlers*. Answers only need to include one source of stress.

14. Helping families find resources and information about a topic that interests them is discussed on pages 353–354 of *Caring for Infants & Toddlers*. Answers only need to include one example.

Multiple Choice

15. b

16. d

Extended Answer

17. Planning and preparing for conferences is discussed on pages 349–352 of *Caring for Infants & Toddlers*. In their answers, teachers should include flexible scheduling of conferences, reviewing and summarizing information they have collected about each child's progress, organizing portfolio samples to share, thinking about their goals for the child, and encouraging families to consider family goals for the conference.

18. Family participation in classroom activities is discussed on pages 344–348 of *Caring for Infants & Toddlers*. Answers should include a specific example of one of the many ways that families can be involved and describe at least two strategies for making the experience meaningful for families.

Module 12: Program Management

Matching

1. b

2. c

3. d

4. a

Fill in the Blank

5. Useful observation notes are complete, accurate, and objective.

6. A program should have a written curriculum to guide teachers' work and a system of ongoing assessment to determine how each child is progressing.

7. Reasons why teachers observe children are discussed on pages 369–371 of *Caring for Infants & Toddlers*. Answers should include at least two of these reasons: to determine each child's skills, interests, and needs; to document and report progress; to get information to share with children's families; to plan ways to support each child's development and learning; and to evaluate the effectiveness of the environment and practices. Any other reasonable answer may also be accepted.

8. Children do not behave the same way all of the time, so a single observation cannot provide a complete picture of a child. Many factors affect what children do and say, and children change over time, so observation is an ongoing process.

Short Answer

9. Portfolio items are listed on page 377 of *Caring for Infants & Toddlers*.

10. Answers need to list two sources of information: the child, the child's family, doctors, specialists, the child's previous teachers, books, journals, the Internet, regional and national support groups, and clearinghouses.

11. Items to include in weekly planning are discussed on page 386 of *Caring for Infants & Toddlers*. There is a sample weekly planning form on page 387.

Multiple Choice

12. c

13. b

Extended Answer

14. Daily evaluation questions are discussed on pages 388–389 of *Caring for Infants & Toddlers*.

15. Team members each bring different strengths, interests, perspectives, and resources to planning and evaluation. The more all team members are involved in planning and evaluation, the more likely they are to realize their important role in providing a high-quality program.

Module 13: Professionalism

Matching

1. d

2. a

3. b

4. c

Fill in the Blank

5. A professional is a person who has specialized knowledge and skills.

6. Advocacy means working for a cause (or working for change).

7. NAEYC issues position statements in order to improve public policies affecting early childhood programs. NAEYC also issues position statements that describe ways to improve early childhood program practices.

8. A teacher at the survival stage would be concerned about immediate needs such as learning the program's routines and performing assigned tasks.

9. There are many correct answers. Ethical responsibilities that early childhood professionals have to their co-workers include treating colleagues respectfully; being honest, dependable, and regular in attendance; dressing appropriately for work; and advocating on behalf of teachers and high-quality early childhood programs.

Short Answer

10. Ways for teachers to continue to grow and learn professionally are discussed on pages 409–411 of *Caring for Infants & Toddlers*. These include joining professional organizations and taking advantage of the print and video materials they offer, reading information on the Internet, joining a study group, attending professional conferences, and participating in training or degree programs. Answers need to identify two of these ways.

11. Ways for teachers to advocate for children and early childhood programs are listed on pages 417–418 of *Caring for Infants & Toddlers*. Answers only need to include one of these ways.

12. *Caring for Infants & Toddlers* describes the work of early childhood professional organizations on pages 401–403 and in the chart on pages 407–408. Answers should name one of these organizations and include at least one of its resources. Answers need not be extensive.

13. Teachers should work to bring about collaboration between families and the program in ways that enhance each child's development. Answers might address the way that teachers speak with families, maintain confidentiality, offer support when families are stressed, and jointly find solutions when conflicts arise.

Multiple Choice

14. b

15. d

Extended Answer

16. There are many correct answers. Change is not possible without awareness and understanding, and teachers are in a good position to help others understand the important issues and concerns of the early childhood field. Teachers know a lot about the value of high-quality care and education, children's developmental needs, and the kind of early childhood environments that support children's growth and learning.

17. Pages 409–411 of *Caring for Infants & Toddlers* includes an extensive discussion of ways that teachers can continue learning about their field and their work with children. Answers should include two strategies that the teacher found to be effective and a discussion of why the strategies were helpful.

Competency Assessment

Teacher: _____ **Observer:** _____

Date/Time: _____ **Setting:** _____

Review your records from this observation and other information you collected while this teacher was working on module 1. Score each criterion of competence that you can substantiate.

Maintaining Practices and Environments That Prevent and Reduce Injuries

The competent teacher will:

check the appropriate box — met / partially met / not met

	met	partially met	not met
1. Check indoor and outdoor areas, toys, materials, and equipment daily and address identified hazards.	☐	☐	☐
2. Keep potentially dangerous items and substances out of children's reach at all times.	☐	☐	☐
3. Check safety equipment monthly to ensure that it is in good condition and easy for adults to reach.	☐	☐	☐
4. Arrange the room with clear exits, pathways, and areas where children can move without bumping into anything.	☐	☐	☐
5. Work with colleagues to supervise all children at all times.	☐	☐	☐

Planning for and Responding to Emergencies

The competent teacher will:

check the appropriate box — met / partially met / not met

	met	partially met	not met
6. Maintain current medical information for all children.	☐	☐	☐
7. Respond quickly and calmly to children in distress.	☐	☐	☐
8. Develop and post injury and emergency procedures and evacuation routes.	☐	☐	☐
9. Make sure a telephone is easy to reach and working properly.	☐	☐	☐
10. Check the first-aid kit and safety devices regularly and restock or repair them as needed.	☐	☐	☐
11. Know and follow established procedures for taking children to safety during fire and other hazard drills and in real emergencies.	☐	☐	☐

Showing Children That They Are in a Safe Place

The competent teacher will:

check the appropriate box   *met*   *partially met*   *not met*

12. Explain to children what you are doing while taking safety precautions.   ☐ ☐ ☐

13. Use positive guidance strategies to redirect children from unsafe to safe activities.   ☐ ☐ ☐

14. Model ways to stay safe throughout the day.   ☐ ☐ ☐

15. Introduce a few important safety rules to toddlers.   ☐ ☐ ☐

16. Share information with families so they can promote their children's safety.   ☐ ☐ ☐

Competency Assessment

Teacher:	Observer:
Date/Time:	Setting:

Review your records from this observation and other information you collected while this teacher was working on module 2. Score each criterion of competence that you can substantiate.

Creating and Maintaining Indoor and Outdoor Environments That Promote Wellness

The competent teacher will:

check the appropriate box — met / partially met / not met

1. Check the room daily for adequate ventilation and lighting, comfortable temperatures, and sanitary conditions. ☐ ☐ ☐

2. Arrange the diapering area so it is easy to sanitize. ☐ ☐ ☐

3. Provide tissues and paper towels where mobile infants and toddlers can reach them. ☐ ☐ ☐

4. Complete daily health checks and stay alert to symptoms of illness throughout the day. ☐ ☐ ☐

5. Wash and disinfect toys and surfaces daily. ☐ ☐ ☐

6. Use the handwashing methods recommended by the American Academy of Pediatrics (AAP) and the American Public Health Association (APHA) to help prevent the spread of germs. ☐ ☐ ☐

Using Daily Routines to Introduce Good Health and Nutrition to Infants and Toddlers

The competent teacher will:

check the appropriate box — met / partially met / not met

7. Help children gradually gain self-help skills for toileting, handwashing, toothbrushing, and eating. ☐ ☐ ☐

8. Model and talk about healthy habits such as handwashing, using tissues, eating nutritious foods, and washing and disinfecting materials and surfaces. ☐ ☐ ☐

9. Tell families about how you and your colleagues promote wellness. ☐ ☐ ☐

10. Exchange information with families about their child's health and nutrition. ☐ ☐ ☐

From *Trainer's Guide to Caring for Infants & Toddlers.*
©2005 Teaching Strategies, Inc., Washington, DC 20015; www.TeachingStrategies.com

Recognizing and Reporting Child Abuse and Neglect

The competent teacher will:

check the appropriate box   *met*   *partially met*   *not met*

11. Respond to children in caring ways while avoiding situations that might be questioned by others.

12. Know the definitions of physical abuse, physical neglect, sexual abuse, and emotional abuse and neglect.

13. Recognize and be alert to the physical and behavioral signs that a child might be a victim of abuse or neglect.

14. Report suspected child abuse and neglect to authorities according to applicable laws and program policies.

15. Support families by helping them get the services they need.

Competency Assessment

Teacher: _____   **Observer:** _____

Date/Time: _____   **Setting:** _____

Review your records from this observation and other information you collected while this teacher was working on module 3. Score each criterion of competence that you can substantiate.

Creating Indoor and Outdoor Spaces That Support Relationships and Encourage Exploration

The competent teacher will:

check the appropriate box — met / partially met / not met

1. Establish areas for different kinds of play and for diapering, feeding, and other routines. ☐ ☐ ☐

2. Create a relaxed, homelike atmosphere. ☐ ☐ ☐

3. Include open areas where children can safely move and explore. ☐ ☐ ☐

4. Make changes to the environment, if necessary, to support children with disabilities. ☐ ☐ ☐

5. Arrange the outdoor area to support a variety of activities. ☐ ☐ ☐

Selecting and Arranging Equipment and Materials That Promote Development and Learning

The competent teacher will:

check the appropriate box — met / partially met / not met

6. Provide materials that include the cultures and languages of the children and their families. ☐ ☐ ☐

7. Provide a variety of open-ended materials that can be used safely in different ways. ☐ ☐ ☐

8. Offer materials that encourage children to use their senses. ☐ ☐ ☐

9. Arrange play materials so children can find and return them on their own. ☐ ☐ ☐

10. Display materials so children can choose them without being overwhelmed or frustrated. ☐ ☐ ☐

Planning Daily Routines and a Flexible Schedule That Meet Each Child's Needs

The competent teacher will:

check the appropriate box — met / partially met / not met

11. Allow ample time for completing daily routines. ☐ ☐ ☐

12. Follow a consistent but flexible schedule that can be adapted to respond to individual and group needs. ☐ ☐ ☐

13. Plan time each day for the children to be outdoors. ☐ ☐ ☐

14. Help each child relax and feel comfortable at naptime. ☐ ☐ ☐

15. Communicate often with families about their children. ☐ ☐ ☐

Competency Assessment

Teacher: _____ **Observer:** _____

Date/Time: _____ **Setting:** _____

Review your records from this observation and other information you collected while this teacher was working on module 4. Score each criterion of competence that you can substantiate.

Creating Indoor and Outdoor Environments That Invite Infants and Toddlers to Move and Explore

The competent teacher will:

check the appropriate box — met / partially met / not met

1. Use furniture, platforms, and ramps to create multiple levels. ☐ ☐ ☐

2. Provide a variety of surfaces on which children can lie, roll, crawl, walk, and use wheeled toys. ☐ ☐ ☐

3. Offer safe and interesting objects and materials that invite children to explore with their senses. ☐ ☐ ☐

4. Provide toys and materials that invite children to use their hands and fingers, such as squeeze balls, rattles, and pop beads. ☐ ☐ ☐

5. Provide a variety of equipment and materials that invite children to use their arms and legs. ☐ ☐ ☐

Offering Opportunities for Infants and Toddlers to Use Their Muscles

The competent teacher will:

check the appropriate box — met / partially met / not met

6. Schedule outdoor play twice a day (in full-day programs). ☐ ☐ ☐

7. Provide opportunities for indoor active play during bad weather. ☐ ☐ ☐

8. Provide materials and activities for children with different levels of fine and gross motor skills. ☐ ☐ ☐

9. Invite children to participate in routines so they can develop and use self-help skills. ☐ ☐ ☐

10. Offer music and movement activities so children can move their bodies and become aware of rhythm. ☐ ☐ ☐

Responding as Infants and Toddlers Practice and Gain New Physical Skills

The competent teacher will:

check the appropriate box — met / partially met / not met

11. Observe, record, and exchange information with families about each child's physical abilities, interests, and needs. ☐ ☐ ☐

12. Share children's pleasure in their new accomplishments. ☐ ☐ ☐

13. Recognize and respect each child's individual rate of development. ☐ ☐ ☐

14. Ensure safety by adapting the environment and teaching practices as children gain new skills. ☐ ☐ ☐

Competency Assessment

Teacher: _____ **Observer:** _____

Date/Time: _____ **Setting:** _____

Review your records from this observation and other information you collected while this teacher was working on module 5. Score each criterion of competence that you can substantiate.

Creating an Environment That Invites Infants and Toddlers to Learn by Using Their Senses and Moving Their Bodies

The competent teacher will:

check the appropriate box — met / partially met / not met

1. Organize the room to help children develop a sense of order. ☐ ☐ ☐
2. Include a variety of interesting things for children to touch, taste, see, hear, and smell. ☐ ☐ ☐
3. Offer open-ended materials that children can use in different ways according to their skills and interests. ☐ ☐ ☐
4. Provide toys and materials that allow infants and toddlers to begin to understand that their actions cause results. ☐ ☐ ☐
5. Provide places and equipment that encourage infants and toddlers to move their bodies. ☐ ☐ ☐

Offering Opportunities for Infants and Toddlers to Explore and Begin to Understand Their World

The competent teacher will:

check the appropriate box — met / partially met / not met

6. Invite children to participate in daily routines so they feel competent and learn how things work. ☐ ☐ ☐
7. Take children outdoors and into the neighborhood. ☐ ☐ ☐
8. Create opportunities for children to touch, taste, see, hear, and smell. ☐ ☐ ☐
9. Encourage children to experiment, make discoveries, and think. ☐ ☐ ☐

Interacting With Infants and Toddlers in Ways That Encourage Them to Explore

The competent teacher will:

check the appropriate box — met / partially met / not met

10. Identify and respond to individual children's interests, needs, and learning styles. ☐ ☐ ☐
11. Talk with children about what they are touching, tasting, seeing, hearing, smelling, and doing. ☐ ☐ ☐
12. Share in children's pleasure and excitement about their explorations, discoveries, and accomplishments. ☐ ☐ ☐
13. Introduce words that describe children's experiences and discoveries. ☐ ☐ ☐
14. Recognize when to let children solve problems on their own and when to offer help. ☐ ☐ ☐
15. Answer children's questions and encourage them to ask more. ☐ ☐ ☐
16. Tell families about their children's use of thinking skills. ☐ ☐ ☐

From *Trainer's Guide to Caring for Infants & Toddlers.*
©2005 Teaching Strategies, Inc., Washington, DC 20015; www.TeachingStrategies.com

Competency Assessment

Teacher: _____ **Observer:** _____

Date/Time: _____ **Setting:** _____

Review your records from this observation and other information you collected while this teacher was working on module 6. Score each criterion of competence that you can substantiate.

Creating Places Where Infants and Toddlers Can Enjoy Sounds, Language, Pictures, and Print

The competent teacher will:

check the appropriate box — met / partially met / not met

1. Provide pleasant sounds and music when children are likely to listen. ☐ ☐ ☐

2. Include a variety of books that correspond to individual and group skills, interests, languages, cultures, and families. ☐ ☐ ☐

3. Make books about familiar people, objects, and events and share them with children. ☐ ☐ ☐

4. Provide inviting, comfortable, cozy spaces for communicating with one child or a small group. ☐ ☐ ☐

5. Provide toys, materials, and equipment that encourage talking and playing together. ☐ ☐ ☐

6. Share pictures and photographs of familiar objects, events, and people, including children's families. ☐ ☐ ☐

Offering Opportunities for Infants and Toddlers to Explore Sounds, Language, Pictures, and Print

The competent teacher will:

check the appropriate box — met / partially met / not met

7. Use pictures and word labels to show where toys and materials are stored. ☐ ☐ ☐

8. Encourage children to notice sounds in their indoor and outdoor environments. ☐ ☐ ☐

9. Provide a variety of papers and writing tools for children who are ready for them. ☐ ☐ ☐

10. Introduce new and interesting sounds, words, and language patterns. ☐ ☐ ☐

11. Read aloud every day, with individual infants and very small groups of toddlers. ☐ ☐ ☐

12. Encourage families to read aloud. ☐ ☐ ☐

13. Model reading and writing during daily routines. ☐ ☐ ☐

Encouraging and Responding to Infants' and Toddlers' Efforts to Communicate

The competent teacher will:

check the appropriate box — met · partially met · not met

14. Listen and respond to children's gestures, vocalizations, words, and phrases. ☐ ☐ ☐

15. Talk with children about what they see and experience throughout the day. ☐ ☐ ☐

16. Learn a few important words in families' home languages so that the children know that their home language is important to you. ☐ ☐ ☐

17. Share enjoyment of listening, talking, singing, reading, and writing. ☐ ☐ ☐

18. Make comments and pose questions that encourage children to communicate. ☐ ☐ ☐

From *Trainer's Guide to Caring for Infants & Toddlers.*
©2005 Teaching Strategies, Inc., Washington, DC 20015; www.TeachingStrategies.com

Competency Assessment

Teacher: _____   **Observer:** _____

Date/Time: _____   **Setting:** _____

Review your records from this observation and other information you collected while this teacher was working on module 7. Score each criterion of competence that you can substantiate.

Creating an Environment That Encourages Exploration and Experimentation

The competent teacher will:

check the appropriate box — met | partially met | not met

1. Create safe, open spaces where infants and toddlers can explore freely.   ☐ ☐ ☐
2. Designate areas with a washable floor and surfaces for messy play and meals.   ☐ ☐ ☐
3. Offer a variety of open-ended materials.   ☐ ☐ ☐
4. Invite children to notice and appreciate interesting and beautiful things.   ☐ ☐ ☐
5. Model creativity by solving problems, being resourceful, and trying new ideas.   ☐ ☐ ☐

Offering Opportunities for Children to Do Things in Unique Ways

The competent teacher will:

check the appropriate box — met | partially met | not met

6. Follow a flexible schedule so children can do things in their own ways and at their own paces.   ☐ ☐ ☐
7. Offer messy, open-ended activities such as sand and water play, painting, and making and using playdough.   ☐ ☐ ☐
8. Include play materials, props, music, books, and other items that reflect the families, cultures, and ethnicities of all children in the group.   ☐ ☐ ☐
9. Encourage sensory exploration during routines and activities.   ☐ ☐ ☐
10. Play make-believe games with children.   ☐ ☐ ☐

Appreciating Each Child's Way of Being Creative

The competent teacher will:

check the appropriate box — met | partially met | not met

11. Respond to and build on children's efforts to communicate.   ☐ ☐ ☐
12. Get involved in children's play by following and responding to their cues.   ☐ ☐ ☐
13. Describe children's use of creative thinking to solve a problem.   ☐ ☐ ☐
14. Respect children's concentration.   ☐ ☐ ☐
15. Share with families examples of their children's creative thinking and learning.   ☐ ☐ ☐

Competency Assessment

Teacher: _____   **Observer:** _____

Date/Time: _____   **Setting:** _____

Review your records from this observation and other information you collected while this teacher was working on module 8. Score each criterion of competence that you can substantiate.

Helping Children Learn About Themselves and Others

The competent teacher will:

		check the appropriate box	met	partially met	not met
1.	Include family photos and familiar items that help children feel connected to home while they are at the program.		☐	☐	☐
2.	Include books, decorations, music, and other items that reflect the cultures of all of the children and teachers.		☐	☐	☐
3.	Provide multiples of popular play materials so children do not have to share or take turns before they are ready.		☐	☐	☐
4.	Arrange the furniture, materials, and equipment so mobile infants and toddlers can do things on their own when they are ready.		☐	☐	☐
5.	Learn and use a few words, songs, and rhymes in the home languages of children whose home language is not English.		☐	☐	☐

Providing Experiences That Allow Children to Be Successful

The competent teacher will:

		check the appropriate box	met	partially met	not met
6.	Provide a range of activities and materials that can be enjoyed by children with varied skills, abilities, and interests.		☐	☐	☐
7.	Acknowledge children's efforts as well as their accomplishments.		☐	☐	☐
8.	Invite children to participate in daily routines to the extent that their abilities and interests allow, even if they take a long time.		☐	☐	☐
9.	Accept mistakes as a natural part of learning.		☐	☐	☐
10.	Repeat activities so children can master skills and experience success.		☐	☐	☐

Building Supportive Relationships With Individual Children

The competent teacher will:

check the appropriate box — met / partially met / not met

11. Observe each child regularly to learn about individual needs, skills, abilities, interests, culture, and family experiences. ☐ ☐ ☐

12. Offer verbal and gentle nonverbal contact to show you care about a child's well-being. ☐ ☐ ☐

13. Identify and respond to children's needs and emotions with respect and empathy. ☐ ☐ ☐

14. Help children cope with their feelings about separating from and reuniting with their family members. ☐ ☐ ☐

15. Spend individual time playing, laughing, and talking with each child, every day. ☐ ☐ ☐

Competency Assessment

Teacher: _____ **Observer:** _____

Date/Time: _____ **Setting:** _____

Review your records from this observation and other information you collected while this teacher was working on module 9. Score each criterion of competence that you can substantiate.

Creating an Environment That Helps Children Develop Social Skills

The competent teacher will: check the appropriate box — met / partially met / not met

1. Provide play materials that can be used by more than one child at a time. ☐ ☐ ☐
2. Encourage children to be helpful. ☐ ☐ ☐
3. Include simple, homelike props that encourage beginning forms of pretend play. ☐ ☐ ☐
4. Provide duplicates of popular items so children can play without having to share. ☐ ☐ ☐
5. Respond to children's communications. ☐ ☐ ☐

Providing Opportunities for Children to Enjoy and Appreciate Other People

The competent teacher will: check the appropriate box — met / partially met / not met

6. Plan daily jobs so one or two children can work together with a teacher. ☐ ☐ ☐
7. Use routines as opportunities to interact with individual children. ☐ ☐ ☐
8. Play with children to model social and pretending skills. ☐ ☐ ☐
9. Involve children in simple activities that involve cooperation. ☐ ☐ ☐
10. Help children value the contributions of others. ☐ ☐ ☐

Helping Children Get Along With Each Other

The competent teacher will: check the appropriate box — met / partially met / not met

11. Pay attention to children's expressions of feelings and respond appropriately to show them how to get along with others. ☐ ☐ ☐
12. Introduce spoken language children can use to express what they want and how they feel. ☐ ☐ ☐
13. Model ways to express feelings by sharing your own. ☐ ☐ ☐
14. Explain how another child might be feeling. ☐ ☐ ☐
15. Help children learn how to treat others well. ☐ ☐ ☐

From *Trainer's Guide to Caring for Infants & Toddlers.*
©2005 Teaching Strategies, Inc., Washington, DC 20015; www.TeachingStrategies.com

Competency Assessment

Teacher: _____ **Observer:** _____

Date/Time: _____ **Setting:** _____

Review your records from this observation and other information you collected while this teacher was working on module 10. Score each criterion of competence that you can substantiate.

Providing an Environment That Supports the Development of Self-Control

The competent teacher will:

	check the appropriate box	met	partially met	not met
1. Provide safe, well-organized spaces that let children make choices and use materials.		☐	☐	☐
2. Follow a flexible schedule so teachers can respond promptly to children's needs.		☐	☐	☐
3. Plan daily routines and activities to minimize waiting time.		☐	☐	☐
4. Create visible, cozy areas where a child, or a child and a teacher, can spend time alone.		☐	☐	☐
5. Prepare children for changes and transitions.		☐	☐	☐

Helping Children Understand and Manage Their Feelings

The competent teacher will:

	check the appropriate box	met	partially met	not met
6. Teach children words to name their feelings.		☐	☐	☐
7. Model appropriate ways to identify and express feelings.		☐	☐	☐
8. Read books, tell stories, and talk about feelings.		☐	☐	☐
9. Accept and respond to the feelings expressed through crying, words, other vocal sounds, and gestures.		☐	☐	☐
10. Offer materials and activities that may calm and soothe children who are upset.		☐	☐	☐

Using Positive Guidance to Help Children Gain Self-Control

The competent teacher will:

	check the appropriate box	met	partially met	not met
11. Get to know and understand each child's temperament.		☐	☐	☐
12. Use simple, positive statements that tell children what to do, rather than only what not to do.		☐	☐	☐
13. Redirect children from unwanted to acceptable behavior.		☐	☐	☐
14. Anticipate problem behaviors and take steps to prevent them.		☐	☐	☐
15. Look for the reasons behind a child's problem behavior.		☐	☐	☐

From *Trainer's Guide to Caring for Infants & Toddlers.*
©2005 Teaching Strategies, Inc., Washington, DC 20015; www.TeachingStrategies.com

Competency Assessment

Teacher: _____ **Observer:** _____

Date/Time: _____ **Setting:** _____

Review your records from this observation and other information you collected while this teacher was working on module 11. Score each criterion of competence that you can substantiate.

Developing a Caregiving Partnership With Each Family

The competent teacher will:

	check the appropriate box	met	partially met	not met
1.	Exchange positive and current information about each child's routines and activities every day.	☐	☐	☐
2.	Invite and respond to families' questions and concerns.	☐	☐	☐
3.	Get to know a little about each family.	☐	☐	☐
4.	Use information provided by families to meet individual needs.	☐	☐	☐
5.	Plan jointly with families to offer children consistency and security at home and at the program.	☐	☐	☐

Offering a Variety of Ways for Families to be Involved in the Program

The competent teacher will:

	check the appropriate box	met	partially met	not met
6.	Encourage families to visit the program at any time.	☐	☐	☐
7.	Invite families to share their talents, interests, home languages, and aspects of their cultures.	☐	☐	☐
8.	Offer a variety of family-involvement opportunities to accommodate individual schedules, interests, and skills.	☐	☐	☐
9.	Hold meetings and events at times that are convenient for most families.	☐	☐	☐
10.	Offer workshops and resources on topics of interest to families.	☐	☐	☐

Providing Support to Families

The competent teacher will:

	check the appropriate box	met	partially met	not met
11.	Maintain confidentiality about children and families.	☐	☐	☐
12.	Recognize when families are under stress and offer additional support.	☐	☐	☐
13.	Encourage families to relax and enjoy their children.	☐	☐	☐
14.	Help families recognize what their children learn through daily routines and activities.	☐	☐	☐
15.	Share information about child development and typical behaviors of infants and toddlers.	☐	☐	☐
16.	Use familiar terms, instead of professional jargon, when communicating with families.	☐	☐	☐
17.	Notify a supervisor when a family seems to need professional help.	☐	☐	☐

From *Trainer's Guide to Caring for Infants & Toddlers.*
©2005 Teaching Strategies, Inc., Washington, DC 20015; www.TeachingStrategies.com

Competency Assessment

Teacher: _____ **Observer:** _____

Date/Time: _____ **Setting:** _____

Review your records from this observation and other information you collected while this teacher was working on module 12. Score each criterion of competence that you can substantiate.

Learning About Each Child

The competent teacher will:

check the appropriate box — met / partially met / not met

1. Communicate with families often, using a variety of strategies. ☐ ☐ ☐
2. Observe children regularly and note your observations. ☐ ☐ ☐
3. Observe children in a variety of settings and at different times of the day. ☐ ☐ ☐
4. Collect examples and photographs that document children's skills, interests, and progress. ☐ ☐ ☐
5. Take advantage of everyday routines and interactions to learn about children's interests and abilities. ☐ ☐ ☐

Working as a Team to Offer a Program That Meets Each Child's Needs

The competent teacher will:

check the appropriate box — met / partially met / not met

6. Meet regularly with colleagues to plan the program. ☐ ☐ ☐
7. Ensure that curriculum goals are the basis for planning experiences for the children. ☐ ☐ ☐
8. Use ongoing assessment information to plan for individual children and the group. ☐ ☐ ☐
9. Include each family in planning ways to support their child's development and learning. ☐ ☐ ☐
10. Use creative thinking skills, such a brainstorming, to plan and to solve problems. ☐ ☐ ☐
11. Appreciate and use the strengths of all team members, including teachers, families, and volunteers. ☐ ☐ ☐

Evaluating the Program

The competent teacher will:

check the appropriate box — met / partially met / not met

12. Use program goals as a component of program evaluation. ☐ ☐ ☐
13. Identify what is working well and what needs to be improved, every day. ☐ ☐ ☐
14. Use assessment information to plan teaching approaches and to change the environment, interactions, routines, and activities in response to children's individual characteristics. ☐ ☐ ☐
15. Use information about children's use of materials to determine whether changes are needed. ☐ ☐ ☐

Appendix

Module-Completion Plan

Review your responses to the *Self-Assessment* with your trainer. What do you think are your strengths, interests, and needs? Decide which areas you would like to work on first. Select three modules to begin with and set target dates for their completion. (Your trainer can let you know how much work is involved for each module.) Record the module titles and target completion dates below. You may also wish to determine a tentative schedule for completing *Caring for Infants & Toddlers*.

Module	Target Completion Date

Tentative schedule for completion of the *Caring for Infants & Toddlers* Training Program:

Module	Date

Teacher:_____ Date:_____ Trainer:_____ Date:_____

From *Trainer's Guide to Caring for Infants & Toddlers*.
©2005 Teaching Strategies, Inc., Washington, DC 20015; www.TeachingStrategies.com

Planning Form for Group Sessions

Module: _____

Use this form to plan a series of group sessions on a module. Tailor your plan to address individual interests and training needs.

Overview, Your Own Experiences, and Pre-Training Assessment

1. Open the session. Greet participants. Return completed forms with your comments and give teachers time to review them. Begin a dialogue by asking an open-ended question.

   _____

   _____

   _____

   _____

   _____

   _____

2. Discuss the module topic.
   Introduce the three areas of competence related to the module topic.

   _____

   _____

   _____

   _____

   _____

   _____

   Lead a discussion by posing questions that will encourage participation.

   _____

   _____

   _____

   _____

   _____

   _____

From *Trainer's Guide to Caring for Infants & Toddlers.*
©2005 Teaching Strategies, Inc., Washington, DC 20015; www.TeachingStrategies.com

Planning Form for Group Sessions, continued

3. Review the three examples in the overview.

    Discuss the example situations and teachers' responses to the questions. Ask participants to describe similar experiences and their own practices. Ask questions such as the following:

    *   What do you think about the way the teacher handled the situation?
    *   How would you handle a similar situation in your program?

    _____

    _____

    _____

    _____

    _____

    _____

    _____

4. Discuss the section on teachers' personal experiences.

    _____

    _____

    _____

    _____

    _____

    _____

5. End the session.

    Answer questions. Schedule individual meetings or phone conferences to discuss responses and the 3–5 skills and topics teachers want to learn more about.

Planning Form for Group Sessions, continued

Learning Activity*:_____

1. Open the session.

    Greet participants. Return completed learning activity forms with your comments and give teachers
    time to review them. Begin a dialogue by asking an open-ended question, reviewing the previous
    learning activity, or discussing a follow-up assignment from the previous meeting.

    _____

    _____

    _____

    _____

    _____

    _____

2. Discuss the text.

    Lead a discussion about the key points presented in the learning activity.

    _____

    _____

    _____

    _____

    _____

    _____

3. Review the activity.

    Ask participants to describe their experiences completing this learning activity. Encourage them to
    share examples from their work with children, families, and colleagues.

    _____

    _____

    _____

    _____

    _____

    _____

* Complete one plan for each learning activity in this module.

From *Trainer's Guide to Caring for Infants & Toddlers.*
©2005 Teaching Strategies, Inc., Washington, DC 20015; www.TeachingStrategies.com

4. Offer additional resources and activities.

   List any materials, audiovisual resources, topics for discussion, or exercises you will use to supplement the learning activity.

   _____

   _____

   _____

   _____

   _____

   _____

5. End the session.

   Introduce the next learning activity.

   _____

   _____

   _____

   _____

   _____

   _____

   Offer to review and discuss the activity during individual meetings or phone conferences.

   Remind participants of the time and place for your next session and when to submit their completed learning activity forms for your review and written comments.

   If this is the last session for this module, also discuss *Reflecting on Your Learning*.

   Return completed progress summaries with your comments. Offer to review and discuss them during individual meetings or phone conferences.

   Ask teachers to share one idea that they learned while working on this module.

   Invite teachers to describe some of the ways they adapted or changed their practices related to the topic addressed in the module.

   Schedule individual meetings with teachers to review their progress and schedule the knowledge and competency assessments.

Individual Tracking Form

Name:_____   Date Completed:_____

Module	Overview	Self-Assessment	Pre-Training Assessment	Your Own Experiences	Learning Activity A	Learning Activity B	Learning Activity C	Learning Activity D	Learning Activity E	Reflecting on Your Learning	Knowledge Assessment	Competency Assessment	Trainer Sign-Off
Orientation	▓		▓	▓	▓	▓	▓	▓	▓			▓	
1. Safe		▓							▓				
2. Healthy		▓							▓				
3. Learning Environment		▓							▓				
4. Physical		▓							▓				
5. Cognitive		▓							▓				
6. Communication		▓							▓				
7. Creative		▓							▓				
8. Self		▓							▓				
9. Social		▓							▓				
10. Guidance		▓							▓				
11. Families		▓							▓				
12. Program Management		▓							▓				
13. Professionalism		▓							▓			▓	

Note: The dark gray boxes indicate sections that are not part of the *Orientation* or of a particular module.

Program Tracking Form

Teachers	Modules																														
	Orientation		Safe		Healthy		Learning Environment		Physical		Cognitive		Communication		Creative		Self		Social		Guidance		Families		Program Management		Professionalism	
	B	C	B	C	B	C	B	C	B	C	B	C	B	C	B	C	B	C	B	C	B	C	B	C	B	C	B	C

B=Begun   **C=Completed**

From *Trainer's Guide to Caring for Infants & Toddlers*.
©2005 Teaching Strategies, Inc., Washington, DC 20015; www.TeachingStrategies.com

Training Record

Name: _____

Program: _____

Topic	Date(s)	Hours	Type of Training (conference, course, workshop, observation/feedback)	Agency Providing Training	Signature of Trainer

From *Trainer's Guide to Caring for Infants & Toddlers.*
©2005 Teaching Strategies, Inc., Washington, DC 20015; www.TeachingStrategies.com

CERTIFICATE of COMPLETION

AWARDED TO

_____

for completion of _____ hours of training on

Caring for Infants & Toddlers, 2nd Edition

_____ 20___

Verification of Training may be obtained from:

Agency Sponsoring Training: _____

Sponsor's Address: _____

City/State/Zip: _____

Sponsor's Phone Number: (___) _____

_____
(Trainer's Signature)

caring for
**infants &
toddlers** second edition

Training Evaluation Form

Session Title:_____ **Date:**_____

Trainer:_____

check the appropriate box — completely / somewhat / not at all

A. Content

1. Did the topics address your needs? ☐ ☐ ☐
2. Was the information relevant to your job? ☐ ☐ ☐

B. Trainer

3. Was the trainer well-informed about the subjects? ☐ ☐ ☐
4. Did the trainer help you learn? ☐ ☐ ☐
5. Was the presentation well-organized? ☐ ☐ ☐

C. Materials

6. How appropriate and usable were the handouts? ☐ ☐ ☐
7. How appropriate were other resources such as videos? ☐ ☐ ☐

D. Suggestions or Comments *(Indicate your likes, dislikes, and recommendations.)*

E. How will you apply what you learned in this training?

Your name (optional): _____

From *Trainer's Guide to Caring for Infants & Toddlers.*
©2005 Teaching Strategies, Inc., Washington, DC 20015; www.TeachingStrategies.com

Notes